MW01678932

A Vocal Invitation to Readers Theatre

Using Readers Theatre to Develop the Child's Voice

by Shirley Konrad

Jj-Otter Read-It™
Educational Resources Ltd.

Canadian Cataloguing in Publication Data

Konrad, Shirley, 1964-
A vocal invitation to readers theatre: using readers theatre to develop the child's voice: a classroom guidebook

Includes bibliographical references and index.
ISBN 0-9681074-4-3

1. Readers' theatre. 2. Voice culture. I. Title.

PN2081.R4K65 2000 808.5'4 C00-900428-9

Published by:
U-Otter-Read-It Educational Resources Ltd.
11 Miller Place
Spruce Grove, Alberta T7X 2N1
Canada

Phone: 780-962-9854
Fax: 780-962-9882
Email: info@uotter.com
Website: www.uotter.com

Editor: Helen Raczuk
Book layout & cover design: Joan Heys Hawkins, Re:Design
Illustrations: Darren Lau

Printed and bound in Canada

Dedication

I dedicate this book to my parents, Frank and Mary Konrad, who, as immigrants from Hungary, valued and respected the need to improve communication skills in order to advance in this country. My parents also intuitively recognized early on the need for intervention in the development of my own speaking skills. I believe that my work in this field has been a calling, and that my path was made clear with their guidance, love, and nurturing support.

Acknowledgments

I acknowledge the support of my family members, and especially my sister, Sue Christensen. Sue, a Speech Pathologist, provided valuable supplemental information and resources on recognition of voice disorders/delays and intervention.

I acknowledge the many friends and colleagues who have given me love, support, and shoulders to lean on — Laurie, Kathy, Ilda, Lee, Stephanie, Ian G., and Souzann.

I am grateful to Helen Raczuk and Marilyn Smith, whose wonderful books inspired me to write further about Readers Theatre. Helen's encouragement, patience, friendship, and knowledge, coupled with Marilyn's creative talents, and their belief in my ability, have truly fostered the creation of this book.

I sincerely thank Joan Heys Hawkins for her positive energy, enthusiasm, and constant support. Her commitment and belief in this project fueled my own excitement and helped turn this book into reality. I also thank Alex Hawkins for his help and encouragement.

Thanks also is extended to a talented student of mine, Darren Lau, whose fabulous drawings have added life and breath to my words and ideas.

To my own speech teacher, Yvonne Hohm: I thank you for introducing Readers Theatre to me, and for being the most inspiring and influential teacher in my life.

I deeply thank the many students with whom I have worked over the past 18 years; they continue to inspire me and give purpose to my life.

And to all those who have journeyed with me on the road less travelled — I thank you.

Shirley Konrad

Table of Contents

Page

The Vital Voice 1

The Voice and Readers Theatre 1
- U-Otter Know This 2
- How To Use This Guidebook 3

The Teacher as a Role Model 5
- The Teacher's Own Voice 5
- Bringing the Text to Life 6
- Tips for Introducing a Poem 7
- A Note about Using Scripts 7

The Child's Voice 8

How the Voice Works 11
- Building Through the Steps of Voice Production . . . 11
- The Instrument 12

Vocal Hygiene 17

Voice Production 19

Relaxation 19

Alignment 25

Breathing 34

Phonation 43

Resonance 47

Articulation 51

Tone Placement and Tone Projection 66

Putting It All Together 72

Table of Contents

Page

Vocal Expression 77

Symbols 77

Pause and Phrasing 78

Pace 84

Pitch 90

Inflection 96

Emphasis 101

Colouring 106

Volume 113

A Vocal Wrap-Up 119

Resources 121

Bibliography 121

Reproducibles 124

U-Otter Get to Know Us!

Shirley Konrad, B.F.A., L.M.R.C., A.R.T.C., A.T.C.L.

As Owner and Director of **The Speech Studio** in Edmonton, Alberta, Shirley has been instrumental in developing the healthy voices of hundreds of students, ranging from three years of age to adults. Shirley teaches privately at her studio, and has taught group instruction at community colleges and schools throughout Alberta, instilling confidence, poise, expressive vocal skills, and dynamic presentational ability in all of the individuals with whom she works. Her innovative and energetic approach to her vocal work has made Shirley a popular festival adjudicator and workshop leader across Canada, and has earned her a position on the College Board of Examiners for the Royal Conservatory of Music (Speech Arts).

Darren Lau

Darren Lau is currently entering Grade 12 at Old Scona Academic High School, and is working toward an International Baccalaureate diploma. Darren's interests include skiing, playing the piano, and doodling in class. This book, however, represents his first *official* work as an illustrator! A student at **The Speech Studio**, Darren has acquired first-hand knowledge of Arty, and the lovable qualities that make him such a unique teaching assistant for Miss Shirley.

Helen K. Raczuk

Helen is a graduate of the University of Alberta, and has done postgraduate work in Illinois, Hawaii, Calgary, and Edmonton.

In the course of her 20+ year career, Helen has been an elementary music specialist, a classroom teacher, the school librarian, a curriculum development committee member with Alberta Education, a home school facilitator, a student teacher facilitator at the University of Alberta, and a content facilitator for developing a web-based educational curriculum.

Helen's passion for children and reading has led her to form a publishing company to develop resources for teachers. **U-Otter-Read-It Educational Resources Ltd.** is the result of both this passion and her friendship with collaborator Marilyn Smith.

When Helen isn't writing or presenting workshops, she can be found singing with the *Richard Eaton Singers*, reading, working in the garden, or baking cookies!

U-Otter-Read-It is based on the belief that learning should be fun. Otters are playful in the way they teach young to swim. In the same way, resources produced by U-Otter-Read-It promote playful, interactive and supportive strategies. Our goal is to produce materials that support teacher planning: are practical, hands-on and ready to use to promote literacy skills at all levels. It is our sincere hope that **A Vocal Invitation to Readers Theatre** will continue to promote the wisdom and sense of fun inherent in the otter.

The Vital Voice

The voice is the most important component of Readers Theatre; the voice gives life to the printed words. Prior to developing Readers Theatre scripts with children, it is vital to understand *how the voice is produced*, and *the effect the voice has on others.*

The Voice and Readers Theatre

Walking and talking are both natural processes. Once a child masters the skill of putting one foot in front of the other while maintaining balance and moving forward, what more needs to be done? Through continued practice, the child improves, and eventually walks without consciously thinking about the process. Similarly, once a child knows how to vocalize coherent words and structured phrases, the vocal process seems to be complete. What more needs to be taught about the voice? ***EVERYTHING!***

The child is only beginning to explore the potential of the voice in these early stages of life. It is up to parents, and eventually teachers, to encourage and promote the child's ability to *use* the voice effectively. Readers Theatre is the perfect vehicle for encouraging a group exploration of the voice.

More than twenty years ago, I was invited to participate in an International Readers Theatre competition in the United States. Up to that time, my exposure to Readers Theatre had been limited. I had worked with a speech arts teacher and some teenagers in small group settings, developing scripts consisting of poetry and prose extracts centered around various themes. Our performance was presented in the conventional style: readers seated on stools, scripts bound in folders, and limited use of physical expression. I remember being confused about what defined Readers Theatre, because the other performance styles I observed at the competition were so varied, creative, and unique. However, in one presentation, the visual components completely overshadowed the text. This experience taught me to define Readers Theatre with this understanding:

> **If you leave a Readers Theatre presentation remembering more of what you've *seen* than what you've *heard*, it isn't Readers Theatre.**

Readers Theatre depends on the VOICE as the primary tool for communicating to the audience.

The voice is the major tool for creating a successful Readers Theatre experience for both the reader and the audience. The voice can:

- Stimulate the imagination
- Set the scenes
- Create the characters
- Stir the emotions
- Capture the moods
- Provoke a response to the text

Our children are becoming *technologically de-voiced*, as computers, email, and video games reduce the need for vocalizing. Due to ever-increasing curriculum demands, the amount of time dedicated to the development of the child's voice is becoming more limited. However, teachers do have the unique opportunity to encourage children to explore their vocal instruments through classroom activities, thereby preventing the onset of undesirable vocal habits. Although few resources are available that support and guide teachers to become comfortable and proficient in this area, awareness is growing.

U-Otter Know This

The main goal of this guidebook is to help the teacher discover how easy it is to explore the *VOICE* through Readers Theatre. **A Vocal Invitation to Readers Theatre** addresses these concerns:

- What kind of exercises develop the strength of the voice so that the child can be heard?
- What are some easy activities for encouraging clear and crisp articulation?
- How can the process of working on the voice be exciting and creative?
- How can children be encouraged to lift the words off the page and into the minds of the listeners?
- How can minor speech problems be addressed?

Understanding the fundamentals of voice production promotes effective communication and encourages expression.

The text is lifted off the page by using the techniques of oral expression. However, if the voice cannot be heard or understood, the effectiveness of expression is lost. Proper vocal habits, encouraged early in children's lives, will have a lasting effect on their speaking skills. For example, simply saying, *"Don't use your shoulders when you breathe"* helps children understand that breathing is supported elsewhere in the body. Warning children not to *scream* as they increase volume eliminates unnecessary and potentially damaging tension on the vocal folds. It is necessary to understand the fundamentals of voice production in order to promote *desirable* vocal habits in children.

Children are open and enthusiastic about exploring their vocal potential. The skills and confidence they develop in the elementary classroom will be invaluable as they enter the upper grade levels where they are required to do more oral presentations and readings. Later, as adults, they will feel comfortable in public speaking or interview situations. The role model sets the standard for healthy vocal habits.

Developing vocal skills in children is a necessary requirement for creating confident adult speakers.

How To Use This Guidebook

The activities in this guidebook have been designed to follow a sequential process. To complement the activities, this guidebook includes Readers Theatre scripts from **U-Otter-Read-It Educational Resources Ltd.** books by Helen Raczuk and Marilyn Smith.

Bibliography, page 121

- **Invitation to Readers Theatre:** *A Guidebook for using Readers Theatre to celebrate holidays and special events throughout the year*
- **Invitation to Munsch:** *A Guidebook for use with selected works of Canadian Author Robert Munsch*
- **Early Literacy — A Seasonal Approach:** *Enhancing a Balanced Literacy Program*

Otter Symbols

Teaching activities

Readers Theatre scripts

Performance ideas

Reproducible pages

Further reading

Important notes

Interesting trivia

Introducing Arty™ and Otter

Articulation, page 51

Arty, the puppet posing with me on the front cover, was created after I realized the need for something to assist with demonstrating the articulators. Prior to this, I had used mirrors and diagrams, although both proved less effective with young children. Mirrors provided some assistance but were cumbersome, and a diagram lacked tangibility. Therefore, I created a child-sized puppet who has a tongue that can be manipulated, an actual soft palate, exaggerated articulators (teeth and lips), and an irresistible personality! My students are completely enthralled with Arty, and I am pleased to introduce him as my teaching assistant.

Arty is presented throughout **A Vocal Invitation to Readers Theatre**, accompanied by Otter, re-created from the Otter symbol found in **U-Otter-Read-It Educational Resources Ltd.** publications.

A Personal Invitation

The ideas provided in this guidebook are intended to serve as a foundation for building mini-lessons and exercises. I invite you to discover how easy it is to explore and develop the child's voice through Readers Theatre.

The Teacher as a Role Model

The Teacher's Own Voice

In the book, **James Earl Jones: Voices and Silences**,[1] James Earl Jones, who was voted by speech and communication experts as having one of the most outstanding voices,[2] talks about experiencing vocal freedom as a child growing up on a farm:

> *"Living on the farm, we always exercised our voices, calling the cows, calling the hogs, never having to worry about bothering neighbors with our sounds."*

About positive feedback and his influences, he says,

> *"Papa used to tell me my child-voice was beautiful, like a bell. I grew up listening to the music of southern voices, the rich oral testimonies guised in stories told on the porch at Papa's or my great-grandfather's house. ... I grew up with the spoken word."*

What children hear in their environments influences the way they speak and express themselves. Children will copy the vocal qualities around them, whether quiet or loud, harsh or gentle. Initially, children imitate the voices of family members. Eventually, they will imitate other voices from their immediate environments, such as those heard on television. Teachers, caregivers, and finally the peer group, all influence the quality of the child's voice.

Model good vocal habits in the classroom.

Modeling is a natural and effective strategy to use in any voice program. Teachers who are aware of their own vocal strengths set a standard for voice quality by what they model, and by which vocal behaviours they encourage. A classroom environment that is rich and positive encourages children to develop healthy, uninhibited voices.

I often ask my students to evaluate the voices they hear in their daily environments — teachers, family members, and friends. They listen closely to the voices, then rate them on six important qualities of an effective voice: flexibility, expressiveness, energy, sincerity, clarity, and pleasantness. The results usually indicate a strong link between favorite subjects and appealing teacher voices. Not surprisingly, teachers who speak in a *monotonic* voice, or who are *boring* in their delivery, are given low scores. How would you rate your own voice? How do you think students would rate your voice?

Qualities of an Effective Voice, page 119

[1] James Earl Jones and Penelope Niven, **James Earl Jones: Voices and Silences**, New York: Macmillan Publishing Co.., 1993, pp29-30.

[2] Lyle V. Mayer, **Fundamentals of Voice and Diction**, 10th Ed., Dubuque, IA: Wm. C. Brown Communications, Inc., 1994, p31.

Teachers model good vocal behaviour and vocal hygiene.

Due to the nature of teaching, and the daily demands it places on the voice, teachers are at high risk of suffering damage to their own vocal instruments. Consider how many teachers lose their voices in September as a result of increased vocal stress, and overuse or improper use of the voice. Teachers can benefit greatly by learning about the vocal instrument, and increasing their personal awareness of vocal hygiene, thus preventing damage and further stress.

Adults model all aspects of voice production, and children naturally imitate what they hear. If an adult mumbles, or lacks clarity, the child will repeat the words, and the result may well be indistinct speech or mispronounciation. Consider the story of a young boy who was participating in a relative's wedding party. As he walked down the aisle, he started to growl at the wedding guests. When asked why he was doing this, he replied, *"I'm the ring-bear!"*

Bringing the Text to Life

Poetry, along with related exercises and activities, is used throughout this guidebook to promote vocal skill development. These tools introduce children to Readers Theatre in a comfortable, imaginative and playful manner.

The teacher serves as a role model to foster the love of poetry.

Once again, the teacher serves as a role model for appreciating and respecting the beauty and depth of poetry. How many adults avoid poetry because, as children, they were introduced to poetry in a less-than-enthusiastic way? Perhaps you are one of those individuals who grew up being intimidated by poetry, or you consider it boring and useless. Too often, the pressure to memorize a poem outweighs any positive experience the poetry can bring. Instilling the joy of language through rhyme, rhythm, and sound leads to a greater appreciation of poetry.

Readers Theatre brings poetry to life.

How the poem is initially heard affects the child's overall appreciation of the experience. Poetry is pleasurable — so have fun with it! Poetry appeals to the senses. The listener and the reader can *feel*, *touch*, *taste*, *see*, and *hear* the various images in their minds. The reader's task, then, is to stimulate the senses of the listeners through oral expression.

Readers Theatre is a way to bring poetry to life, to bring it off the page and into the imaginations of both the speaker and the listener. What better way to approach literature, and to encourage expressive oral reading, than through Readers Theatre?

Tips for Introducing a Poem

Hearing a poem read with expression encourages children to explore their own interpretations. Before working with the class, prepare by studying and experimenting with the poem to determine the most effective way to read it aloud. Being ill-prepared affects the phrasing of the poem and creates a choppy delivery.

Preparation results in effective reading.

Use the following guidelines to introduce a poem effectively:

Prior to reading the poem to children:

- Read the poem aloud several times.
- Explore and develop voices for characters.

During the reading:

- Use expression to further enhance the understanding of the poem.
- Maintain some eye contact with the children to draw them into the selection.

Having the children read the poem aloud:

- Encourage them not to get so caught up in the rhythm of the language that the meaning is lost. Too dominant a rhythm creates an undesirable *sing-song* effect, which lessens the meaning of the words and the impact on the listener. Unfortunately, people often dislike poetry because they associate it with this artificial and deliberate pattern.
- Guide the children in making decisions about using vocal expression techniques, which include pause, pace, pitch, inflection, emphasis, colouring, and volume.

Vocal Expression, page 77

Remember that there is more than one way to read a poem. The text will drive the expression of the poem. It is the task of the reader to make decisions about interpretation; the more confident a reader is, the more sophisticated the interpretation. The teacher's role, then, is to guide and support this process.

Understanding meaning is important to making choices about interpretation and expression.

A Note about Using Scripts

To develop confidence with text, first have the children read the entire script in unison, then divide them into pairs and individual readers. This process requires time for the children to explore voices, characters, reader combinations, and interpretations. Do this over the course of several days to strenghthen confidence and understanding of the text. Once the children have explored the text, add Readers Theatre performance techniques to enhance the presentation.

The Child's Voice

Voice relates to self-esteem.

The voice is a very important element of one's self-esteem. Through vocal expression, we reveal ourselves to other people, and arrive at a better understanding of our own thoughts and feelings.

There is a tendency to stereotype voices, based on our own experiences with different personalities. For example:

- A shrill, grating voice suggests a *tense* and *hyperactive* personality.
- A weak, almost inaudible voice suggests a *shy* and *insecure* personality.

Thus, it is easy to jump to conclusions about a child's personality on the basis of the voice quality. However, as children are encouraged to release their voices, they become more confident and comfortable. This new-found confidence releases them from possible negative stereotypes based on their voice qualities.

Children are often bombarded by instructions that affect their vocal quality, creating barriers that discourage them from reaching their vocal potential. Statements such as *"Don't talk so fast!," "Be quiet!,"* and *"Don't talk with your mouth full!"* are easily interpreted by children as *"Don't **use** your voice."*

Boys and girls receive different messages about what kind of voice is socially acceptable.

Boys are often discouraged from using high-pitched voices because it sounds *unmanly*. The models they imitate tend to be super heroes or big fierce animals, all with voices limited to the lower register.

Girls tend to imitate pop singers, most of whom are sopranos, thus limiting their voices to the upper register. Girls may also imitate high-fashion models, who often speak in wispy, thin, or high voices. Fashion also affects voice production. For example, many girls tend to wear tight belts to hold in their stomachs, and this limits proper breath control.

Girls participating in dance classes tend to develop breathy, weak voices because they are constantly told to *"Suck in the stomach."* They begin to use their throats to project the tone, and develop weak breath support due to the use of the upper chest area instead of the diaphragm.

The elementary classroom provides the ideal environment, and time, to work on the voice and develop the child's vocal potential. Elementary school children naturally enjoy experimenting with different ways of expressing themselves, and respond positively to the reaction from adults. Inappropriate vocal habits have not yet become ingrained.

Great results occur when the child is given the opportunity to work on the voice in the classroom.

Children who work on their voices through Readers Theatre begin to use their voices more effectively in other situations. They will begin to read with more attention to expression. Positive feedback from the audience — peer group, teachers, and family members — reinforces their efforts to speak well. Greater use of the voice results in greater vocal confidence. Children will seek out opportunities to use their voices by participating in plays, assembly readings, and talent shows.

Response to an individual may be related to the quality of the voice. For example, a teacher may not say directly, *"The fact that your voice is so unusual affects your grades on classroom presentations."* However, poor vocal quality may indirectly influence the response to the message being conveyed, resulting in lower grades. Children will also react to the sound of other children's voices. A child may avoid playing with someone whose voice is excessively loud or uncomfortably grating. An adult will be slower to respond positively to a whiny voice.

The quality of the voice affects the way we respond to what the speaker says.

Inappropriate vocal behaviour may affect an individual's performance in many areas of life. Developing the voice and its potential is an important life skill, since the voice plays a vital role in occupations such as law, sales, business, education, and politics. It is unfortunate when voice quality restricts future options. Remember that:

> **A voice that draws attention to itself, and results in negative listener reactions, is a significant lifetime handicap.**

Negative vocal behaviours that may lead to vocal damage affecting overall voice quality include:

Vocal Hygiene, page 17

- **Very loud talking**
- **Sudden shrieks**
- **Forced laughter**
- **Shouting, cheering, or screaming**
- **Strained singing**
- **Excessive talking**

A teacher is often the first to notice a child experiencing voice difficulties. The teacher may observe that the child's voice appears to differ significantly from what would be expected to be *normal* quality, for example, pitch or volume, in relation to the child's age, gender, and physical size. The child's voice quality will often be described as *unpleasant*, *hoarse*, *monotonal*, or *too nasal*, *too low*, or *too loud*.

Early detection and intervention are important when a teacher suspects that a child is exhibiting voice difficulties.

When a teacher suspects that a child is exhibiting voice difficulties, it is advisable to follow school procedures for referral to a Speech-Language Pathologist, who can then determine whether or not further action is required. Voice difficulties should be not be ignored — **early detection and intervention are the keys to correcting vocal problems.**

My Otter Notes

How the Voice Works

Not so fast, Otter —
You'd better read this section first!

I have clients who are in professions that rely heavily on having an effective voice, such as broadcasting, education, and politics. When I ask them whether or not they are aware of *how* the voice is produced, it is always surprising to hear their responses: *It starts in the brain; I think the vocal folds have something to do with it; You just open the mouth and sound comes out.* To me, this clearly indicates how little is understood about the voice, and the process for developing its potential.

Developing the voice is a sequential process that requires a basic knowledge of the mechanics of voice production. It also requires an understanding of the interrelationships of the various components.

Building Through the Steps

This section provides steps to guide individuals through the process of voice production. Each step is cumulative; for example, if you want to work on Step 3, it is necessary to first understand and practice the concepts of Steps 1 and 2. For example:

- One cannot fully explore ***breathing*** unless the body is physically prepared and responsive. Therefore, ***relaxation*** and ***alignment*** need to be understood and practiced before focusing on breathing.
- ***Resonance*** depends on sound being properly created by the vocal folds. If knowledge of ***phonation*** is not applied, tension occurs in the throat, which negatively affects the sound quality and resonance.
- Since ***projection*** uses energy provided by the muscles of exhalation, it is important to understand ***breathing*** and its relationship to projection.

NOTE: It is very important to follow these steps sequentially.

Remember to build through the following steps:

- ☐ Step 1: Relaxation
- ☐ Step 2: Alignment
- ☐ Step 3: Breathing
- ☐ Step 4: Phonation
- ☐ Step 5: Resonance
- ☐ Step 6: Articulation
- ☐ Step 7: Tone Placement
- ☐ Step 8: Tone Projection

The Instrument

Because the mechanics of a voice share common characteristics with the sound production of musical instruments, I will refer to the voice as an *instrument* throughout this guidebook.

The body is to the voice as the sounding board is to the piano.

Compare the voice to a piano. In order to produce good sound, it is important to begin with a finely tuned instrument. If it is out of tune, the sound is flat, distorted, and unpleasant. If the *sounding board* is damaged, the quality of the performance is affected. In the same way, if the body is *out of tune* — that is, unhealthy, tense, or awkwardly positioned — the voice produced may be flat, distorted, and unpleasant. The first two steps of voice production focus on preparing the body as it relates to the voice.

STEP 1

Relaxation, page 19

Step 1: RELAXATION

A ***free voice*** is a voice that is produced with *ease*; a voice that can take on various colours of emotion and thought; a voice that is filled with personality. The first step towards creating a free voice is to make sure that the individual is ***relaxed***.

Relax the Body! Tension anywhere in the body affects the quality of the voice. Tension is most likely to occur in the upper chest, the shoulders, and the throat.

Relax the Throat! The *vocal folds* are located in the throat. Any tension in the throat affects the voice. Tense vocal folds create high-pitched voices — an undesirable vocal quality.

STEP 2

Alignment, page 25

Step 2: ALIGNMENT

The next step is to ensure that the body is *aligned* properly. When children are asked to stand with *proper posture* rather than *in alignment*, they often stand as stiff as a board. Shoulders become tense, bodies look rigid, and facial muscles tighten. The children look like toy soldiers standing at attention.

Alignment means placing the body in a natural, open position, in which everything *falls into line* comfortably and easily.

Step 3: BREATHING

Once the body is relaxed and aligned, we are ready to begin making sound. Let's go back to the example of the piano. To produce a sound from the piano, the pianist must press the keys. The energy used by the pianist is called the *power source*, which initiates the sound from the instrument.

The power source of the voice is the ***breath***. Too often, the importance of proper breathing is underestimated and disregarded — yet this is one of the most important steps in producing a free, supported, and rich tone.

There is a tendency to place the breath into the upper part of our bodies by filling only the top portion of our lungs. Breath that is held in the clavicular-shoulder area is not desirable for proper voice production. The area needed for optimal voice production is the central area of the body, which we use for abdominal-diaphragmatic breathing, or *central breathing*.

Although breathing is automatic, the amount of air inhaled can be consciously controlled. Breathing deeply is critical for the production of a full voice. To fully understand the process of breathing, *U-Otter* review the information on the next page.

STEP 3

Breathing, page 34

Lungs are not located in the shoulders. Avoid moving the shoulder area when breathing.

Breathing Process, page 14

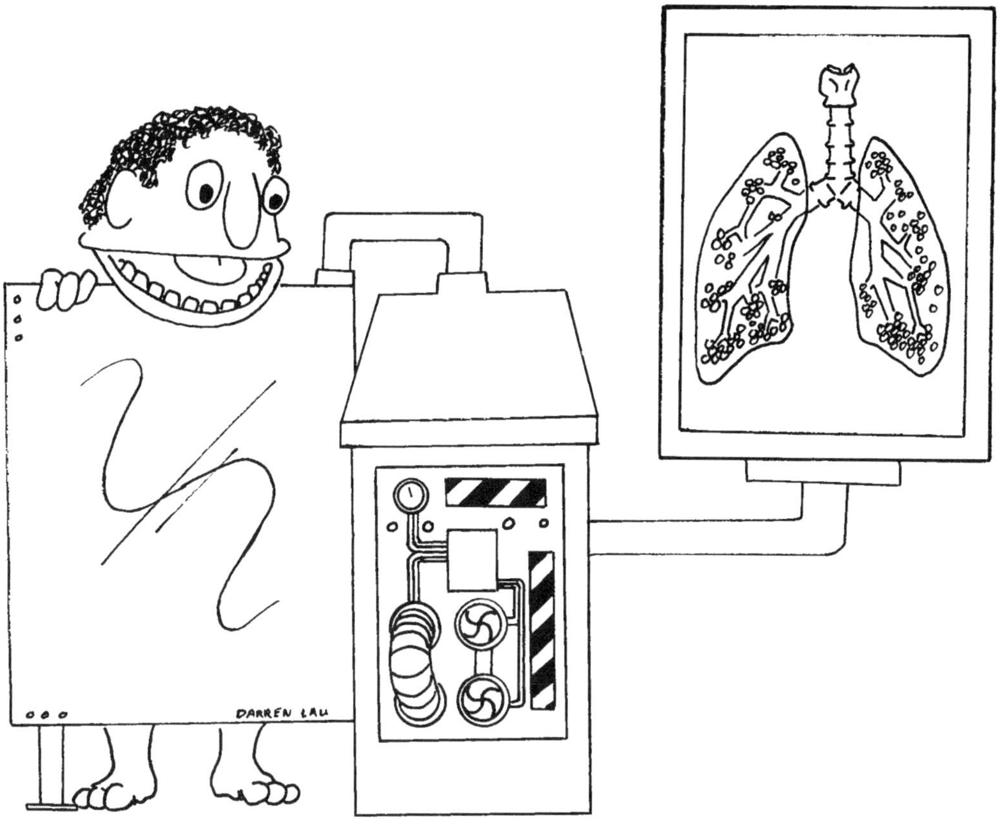

Things U-Otter Know about the Breathing Process

The Breathing Apparatus

- The *lungs* are located in the chest cavity, which is formed by the *ribcage*.
- The ribs are flat bones that are hinged at the spine, curving around to the front of the chest. Most ribs are attached to the breastbone, or *sternum*.
- The tips of the lower ribs are connected by cartilage to the ribs above, and the last two ribs hang free — these are called the *floating ribs*.
- The floor of the chest cavity is formed by the *diaphragm*, which is a strong, dome-shaped muscle separating the chest from the organs in the abdomen.
- When the muscle is relaxed, the diaphragm is curved, but it flattens and contracts to increase the volume of the chest cavity from top to bottom when air enters the lungs.
- As the diaphragm contracts, it pushes against the *abdominal muscles*, which then bulge slightly forward.
- The ribs are flexible and springy; as air is brought into the lungs, the muscles between the ribs help expand the ribs to increase the chest cavity from side to side, and from back to front.
- Air rushes into the lungs to fill this extra space. In regular (normal) breathing, the diaphragm moves down about 1.5 cm (5/8 inch), but in deep breathing, or breathing for speech, the diaphragm may move as much as 7.5 cm (3 inches).

The Process of Breathing — Inhalation and Exhalation

- The *diaphragm*, the *abdomen*, the *ribs*, and the *lungs* work together during the processes of inhalation and exhalation.
- During **inhalation**, the *diaphragm* flattens and contracts, increasing the chest cavity from top to bottom. The *abdomen* is passive during inhalation, bulging slightly forward into a relaxed, rather than a tense position. The *ribs* open the chest cavity from front to back, and from side to side, increasing the room for lung expansion. To equalize the pressure, air is drawn into the *lungs*.
- During **exhalation**, the abdominal muscles contract and pull in — this is called the *abdominal press*. Exhalation pushes the *diaphragm* into its original relaxed position, decreasing the room in the chest cavity. The *ribs* pull in, helping to drive the air out and support the voice. These actions drive the air out of the *lungs*.

Step 4: PHONATION

STEP 4

Phonation, page 43

In the same way that a hammer striking against a string creates a musical pitch on a piano, the breath causes the *vocal folds* to vibrate, which creates a vibrating column of air that we hear as sound. The strings of a guitar vibrate at a certain rate, depending on their thickness, mass, and tension. The rate of vocal fold vibration is determined by these same characteristics.

As breath is exhaled, the air from the lungs travels up the *windpipe* or *trachea*, and passes through the *larynx*, or *voice box*. The larynx is made of tough cartilage, and is located at the top of the trachea. You can see and feel the larynx as the bulge, or *Adam's Apple*, in the front of the neck. Across the center of the larynx are stretched two leathery sheets known as the *vocal folds*. A small triangular gap is between them. Several muscles control the tension on these vocal folds. When the muscles contract, the folds are brought closer together, narrowing the gap. As breath is exhaled, the air rushes between the vocal folds, causing them to vibrate exactly like the reed of a flute or clarinet. The process of producing sound in this area is called ***phonation***.

Step 5: RESONANCE

STEP 5

Resonance, page 47

The vibrations produced by the strings in the piano are amplified inside the cavity of the piano. Consider the difference in sound quality between an upright piano and a grand piano. The larger the cavity, the more space there is for the vibrations to *resound*. Consider a guitar or violin — the hole behind the strings allows the sound to travel throughout the body of the instrument, which reinforces the quality of the vibrations heard. Blocking this hole prevents the sound from moving outward and being clearly heard.

In the same way that these instruments need cavities for amplifying the sound, the body has *cavity resonators*. The initial sound waves produced by the vocal folds are weak, and must be amplified and reinforced by these main cavity resonators:

- Throat
- Mouth
- Nose

Resonance directly affects the quality of sound produced. If the nose is blocked, the voice becomes *denasal*, or unable to produce the *nasal* sounds of **m**, **n**, and **ng**. If the throat is tight, the sound becomes harsh or strident. A proper balance of the main cavity resonators produces a rich vocal quality.

STEP 6

Articulation, page 51

Step 6: ARTICULATION

Articulation is the clarity of speech. To improve articulation, it is necessary to focus on consonant sounds. Speech requires that sounds be controlled and altered, joined together, and separated. This process is influenced by the action of the articulators, or those parts of the mouth used for clear speaking. The articulators are:

- Lips
- Teeth
- Tongue
- Hard palate
- Soft palate
- Jaw

Things U-Otter Know about Consonant Sounds

The various groups of speech sounds are defined by the way they are produced, and are classified as follows:

- ***Stop-plosives*** or ***plosives*** are sounds produced by blocking the flow of air and quickly releasing it to produce an explosive type of sound. The six plosive sounds are:
  b, **p**, **d**, **t**, **g**, and **k**
- ***Fricatives*** are sounds produced by partly blocking the air flow and forcing it through a narrow opening to produce a hissing or buzzing sound. The fricative sounds are:
  th (with or without vocal fold vibration),
  f, **v**, **h**, **s**, **z,** **sh**, and **zh** (as in *measure*)
- ***Blends*** or ***affricatives*** are formed with a plosive and fricative combined together to create one consonant sound. The affricative sounds are:
  ch (tsh) and **j** (dzh)
- ***Glides*** or ***semi-vowels*** are produced by the continuous gliding movement of the articulators from one vowel position to another. The glide sounds are:
  l, **r**, **w**, **wh,** and **y** (initial position as in *yellow*)
- ***Nasals*** are the sounds resonated in the nasal cavity. The three nasal sounds are:
  m, **n**, and **ng**

Step 7: TONE PLACEMENT

Sometimes sounds seem to be blocked because they are placed in the back of the mouth. By *thinking* the sound forward, and directing it to the front of the mouth, the sound quality is enhanced, which improves both projection and clarity.

STEP 7

Tone Placement, page 66

Step 8: TONE PROJECTION

Projection of the voice is closely related to *volume*. *Volume* is the amount or degree of loudness and force appropriate to the mood and the emotion of what is being spoken. *Projection* refers to the placement of the sound in the room, and is achieved by using energy to *catapult* the voice out into the audience. If listeners cannot hear a voice, they cannot respond appropriately, which is discouraging for the reader.

STEP 8

Tone Projection, page 66

When working with scripts, the tendency is to project into the paper, rather than projecting out into the audience. To avoid this, encourage readers to:

- Keep the head in alignment, and raise the script enough to read comfortably without covering the face.
- Be consciously aware of *where* they want to send the voice.
- Focus on their *desire* to send the voice far. When children are excited about the audience and the content of the material they are delivering, they will add energy to the voice and project much farther.
- Use *energy* to direct the voice to that spot. The energy for the voice comes from the muscles of exhalation, specifically the abdominal muscles, which help drive the air out. Pushing the sound from the throat is damaging to the vocal folds, often producing a sore throat.
- Relax and enjoy! Tension in the body created by nerves due to stage fright will block and hold back the voice.

Caution — Avoid pushing the sound from the throat to reach the audience.

Continued awareness, encouragement, and practice helps the children gain confidence in projecting the voice to everyone in the audience.

Vocal Hygiene

The majority of voice problems result from the misuse of the instrument. It is never too early to learn how to take care of the voice through proper vocal hygiene. Teachers need to provide children with the necessary information to ensure proper treatment of the voice. The reproducible on page 124 provides some healthy tips for vocal care.

Page 124

My Otter Notes

Voice Production

It is important to read the first section of this guidebook, ***The Vital Voice***, before starting on this section. The order of information and activities in this section follows the sequence required to build a strong, clear, and supported voice. Remember to build through the following steps:

- Step 1: Relaxation
- Step 2: Alignment
- Step 3: Breathing
- Step 4: Phonation
- Step 5: Resonance
- Step 6: Articulation
- Step 7: Tone Placement
- Step 8: Tone Projection

Building Through the Steps, page 11

Relaxation

STEP 1

The first step toward producing a well-supported voice is to **relax** the body. Heightened tension and effort directly affects the sound of the voice. A tense voice sounds strident, stiff, and unpleasant.

Children become tense for several reasons:

- They doubt their own ability to express their ideas.
- They fear a negative response from peers and others.
- They forget their lines. However, this becomes less of an issue with Readers Theatre, since the children can use a script.
- They lose their place. Fortunately, with Readers Theatre, other readers can pick up lines, which eliminates pressure on the solo speaker.

There is a tendency to generate a great deal of tension in the upper body, neck, and shoulders. Sitting at a desk for an extended period of time restricts physical freedom. *Tension in the upper body places tension into the throat, and affects the use of the vocal folds.*

Tension anywhere in the body affects breathing and vocal production.

When they are tense, children tend to tighten their hands into fists, or fidget nervously with their clothes. This tension is transferred into the arms, shoulders, and neck, affecting *breathing* and *phonation*.

Warming up with relaxation exercises helps to produce a focused, involved, and confident speaker.

Rigid Robots

Clear a space in the classroom, or move to an open area so that the children have room to move freely and easily.

Invite the children to walk around the room like a robot. Notice how the body changes, and how it feels.

- Does this feel comfortable? Is there pain or discomfort?

It may be helpful to guide the children to focus on specific areas, such as knees, shoulders, or arms.

A tense body creates a harsh, strident voice.

Experiment with robot voices. While walking like robots, greet each other with a handshake and a robot greeting.

- How did the voice feel? How did it sound?

Expect responses such as *stiff*, *broken*, *disjointed*, *flat*, and *tight*. Handshakes will be stiff and mechanical. The children will observe that the more tense the body, the more rigid the voice.

Relaxing Rag Dolls

You will need a rag doll for this activity. A large doll works best, because it is easier to observe its movements and actions.

Show the children the rag doll. Try to make the rag doll stand by holding onto the feet. What happens to the doll? Naturally, the doll will flop over wherever your hands are placed for support. Do the same thing, holding the knees, then the waist. Observe what happens to the arms, head, and upper body.

Ask the children to imitate the rag doll when flopped over at the waist. The body must *feel* limp. Standing in one spot, bend at the waist and flop over. Check to see that:

- ☐ Arms are hanging freely and easily.
- ☐ Head is released and hanging loosely.
- ☐ Knees are relaxed and unlocked.

NOTE: When in a flopped-over position, children tend to hold the head up instead of releasing the neck muscles completely.

Circulate throughout the class, gently lifting arms to see if they swing loosely. Touch heads gently, checking for any tension in the neck. If there appears to be tension, ask the child to release it by relaxing the neck muscles.

While remaining in this flopped-over position, say your name or recite a nursery rhyme. How is a limp voice different from the sound of the robot voice? Expect comments such as:

- A limp voice sounds *lazy*, *expressionless*, and *loose*.
- A rigid voice sounds *tight*, *mechanical*, *high-pitched*, and *broken*.

Have the children *slowly* and *smoothly* roll up to a standing position. The head should gently come up last. The neck contains seven bones that need to be stacked up as if they were building blocks. Focus on this building block image while slowly rolling the head up.

Register the sensation of feeling tall and relaxed. Ask the children to recite a nursery rhyme while in this position. They will notice how free and open the voice feels.

Too tense and *too relaxed* are physical extremes. It is the state between these two, but closer to relaxed, that is most desired. In this physical position, the individual is aware, alert, and energized.

Explore the extremes to find the ideal state of relaxation.

Playing with Poetry

Before reading the poem ***The Long Fall List***, by Marilyn Smith, talk with the children about relaxation.

Page 22

Encourage the children to remember a time when they felt relaxed. Was it:

- After school?
- During the summer holidays?
- Looking up at the stars at night?
- Lying in bed in the morning?

What does relaxation feel like? Discuss.

- Does it feel heavy? Tired? Lazy?

Visualization and discussion strengthen self-awareness and understanding.

Invite the children to close their eyes, and re-create the relaxed feeling. Encourage them to breathe deeply, and to relax even further. Ask them to consider the times of the year when we feel relaxed.

- Do we feel most relaxed in the spring? summer? fall? winter?

Read the poem aloud while the children listen with eyes closed. Guide them to visualize the colours, movements, and activities described in the poem. Guide the imagery further by recalling the sounds and temperatures of a typical autumn day: the warm sun, a gentle cool breeze, the sound of leaves falling, or the sound of the rake piling up the dry leaves.

Read the poem again, this time asking the children to stand up and add movements to illustrate the activities described in the poem, such as *raking*, *packing*, and *cleaning*. Compare the energy needed for these activities with the relaxation they experienced on the floor.

Encourage the children to relax completely at the end of the poem, by curling up gently on the floor. Turn out the lights to encourage further relaxation. Imagine being like a bear who will *"sleep 'til spring."*

The Long Fall List

by Marilyn Smith

Reader 1	Summer days have flown by —
Reader 2	So sad, but it is true!
Reader 3	And my parents, well, they've made a list —
ALL	A list of things to do!
Reader 4	Clean up the flower beds,
Reader 3	Roll up the garden hose.
Reader 2	Organize the tool shed,
Reader 1	Pack up summer clothes.
Reader 3	Put away the picnic stuff.
Reader 2	Stack the shorts in drawers.
Reader 4	Bundle all the beach towels —
Reader 1	And that's not all —
ALL	There's more!
Reader 4	Bring in the harvest —
	Pumpkins, beets and peas.
Reader 2	Pickle them and can them,
Reader 3	Fill the pantry, please.
Reader 2	For school, find your backpack.
Reader 1	Clean it out again.
Reader 4	Get paper, books and crayons —
Reader 3	A ruler and some pens.

Reprinted from ***Invitation to Readers Theatre:*** *A Guidebook for using Readers Theatre to celebrate holidays and special events throughout the year,* U-Otter-Read-It © 1997

The Long Fall List, continued

Reader 1	Grab the metal garden rake,
Reader 2	Heap up all the leaves.
Reader 3	Rake and pile and bag them all
Reader 4	Beneath the empty trees.
Reader 3	The list goes on
Reader 1	And on
ALL	And on!!
Reader 2	I'm feeling rather tired.
Reader 4	Just like the bears, I'll sleep 'til spring,
Reader 3	And maybe I'll get fired!

Reprinted from ***Invitation to Readers Theatre:*** *A Guidebook for using Readers Theatre to celebrate holidays and special events throughout the year,* U-Otter-Read-It © 1997

Weight for This!

Have the children lie comfortably in a relaxed position on the floor. Refer to the checklist below to ensure ***proper floor placement***.

Starting with the feet and working towards the head, contrast the feelings of *heavy* and *light*.

- Imagine that the feet are as heavy as boulders. Hold this feeling for five seconds, and then release. *Register this sensation.*
- Now imagine that the feet are as light as balloons, ready to float up to the ceiling. Hold this feeling for five seconds, and then release. *Register this sensation.*
- Continue through the entire body: knees, buttocks, stomach, chest, shoulders, arms, hands and fingers, neck, head and face. *Register these sensations.*

Page 22

Read the poem, ***The Long Fall List***, again, incorporating the feeling of being tired, as experienced in the warm-up activities. This poem is excellent for introducing the concept of releasing physical tension, and is a tool for achieving complete relaxation.

Page 121

Other poems suitable for relaxation activities include:

- ***Fall Is Around Us***, **Early Literacy — A Seasonal Approach**
- ***Lazy Jane***, **Where the Sidewalk Ends**

Checklist for Proper Floor Placement

Checklist for Proper Floor Placement

- ☐ Arms are relaxed at the sides.
- ☐ Legs are uncrossed, and feet and toes are relaxed.
- ☐ Head is comfortably positioned to eliminate tension in the throat.
- ☐ Eyes are closed.
- ☐ Jaw is loose, with tongue relaxed in the mouth.
- ☐ Mind is focused on loosening as many muscles in the body as possible.
- ☐ Shoulder blades are relaxed under the body to allow the back to open as it lengthens along the floor.

Once a complete state of relaxation is achieved, **alignment** can be addressed by exploring how the positioning of the body affects voice production.

Alignment

STEP 2

Once the child understands, and can achieve, a state of relaxation, it is important to address how the placement of the body, or **alignment**, contributes to proper voice production. *Vocal power* and *support* require correct physical positioning of the body.

Alignment versus posture

Although this step addresses posture, use that word sparingly with children. *Proper posture* is often associated with pulling back the shoulders, holding in the stomach, and standing rigidly. Instead, use the word *alignment*, which better defines a body *falling into line*, a position that ensures ease, energy, freedom, and confidence.

The position of the body directly affects voice quality:

- Pulling the body inwards, or slouching, limits the freedom of the chest cavity for breathing.
- Raising the shoulders places tension on the vocal folds.
- Standing tensely, with feet close together, creates a closed and insecure stance, and weakens the ability to project the voice.

Fall in Line

Start this exercise by standing incorrectly in front of the children: stand with legs and feet tight together, knees bent, back rounded, body tilted to one side, and head forced backward. See photo **A**.

The children should see that the position doesn't *look* right. Ask them to guide you into a better standing position. As the children place you into a proper stance, draw attention to the correct placement of the body parts. They will notice that:

- Feet are apart and knees are relaxed.
- Back is straight and shoulders are relaxed.
- Body is balanced with the head at the top of the spine.
- Arms are relaxed at the sides.

Discuss how proper alignment makes an individual appear confident and at ease. See photo **B**.

Have the children demonstrate improper alignment. How does it feel? Ask them to recite a nursery rhyme, and observe how an incorrect body position affects voice quality. Some distortion will be evident in the quality of the sound produced.

Have them adjust themselves slowly until they are standing in proper alignment, then recite the rhyme. Notice that the voice is open, with no distortion.

☐ **Body**
Stand tall and relaxed, with everything falling into proper alignment.

Domi-no-no

It is important to stand with feet slightly apart to achieve proper balance.

Proper balance is maintained when feet are placed parallel to each other, shoulder-width apart.

Have five children stand shoulder-to-shoulder in a straight line, with feet placed tightly together. Ask the child at one end to lean into the next child. This creates a domino effect.

- What happens to the line? Why?

Try the exercise again, this time standing with feet about a foot apart.

- What happens to the line? Why?

Rocking Chair

To be *centered* and balanced, the weight of the body needs to be distributed evenly on the feet, rather than only on the toes or the heels.

Have the children stand a comfortable distance from each other. They will need to have room to rock freely.

☐ **Feet**
Stay in balance by keeping the feet slightly apart, and centering the weight on the balls of the feet.

Standing with feet parallel to each other and slightly apart, rock back and forth on heels and toes, like a rocking chair. Create a gentle rocking motion, being careful not to throw the body forwards and backwards, or to involve the hands.

Slow the pace of the rocking, and gradually limit the range, as balance becomes centered. Eventually, the rocking should subside until the children are completely still.

The Need for Knees

Tension in the knees causes tension elsewhere in the body, affecting the release of the voice.

☐ **Knees**
Keep the knees straight, but not locked.

Have the children stand comfortably in their own space. Remind them to keep the knees straight, but not locked or tense.

Explore the difference between locked knees and relaxed knees. First lock the knees, and then relax them. Repeat the locking and relaxing. What happens?

Tension creates a stiff and flat voice.

Exaggerate the tension in the knees, and then recite a nursery rhyme. Observe how that tension affects voice quality.

Relax the knees and recite the nursery rhyme. What is the difference in voice quality?

Hip, Hip, Hooray

Straightening the lower back reduces tension in the stomach area, and assists with breathing by allowing access to the abdominal muscles.

Introduce the term *banana back*. This is a back that swings out backwards from the hips, creating an arch in the lower back region. See photo **A**. Someone walking in this position would look a bit like a duck. Dancers are particularly susceptible to this position, and need to be taught to avoid a banana back.

Stand in a banana back position. Recite a rhyme.
- What happens to the voice quality?

Now align the back by tucking the hips under the body, and relaxing the stomach muscles. See photo **B**. Recite a rhyme.
- What happens to the voice quality?
- Which position is more comfortable?
- Which position supports a better voice?

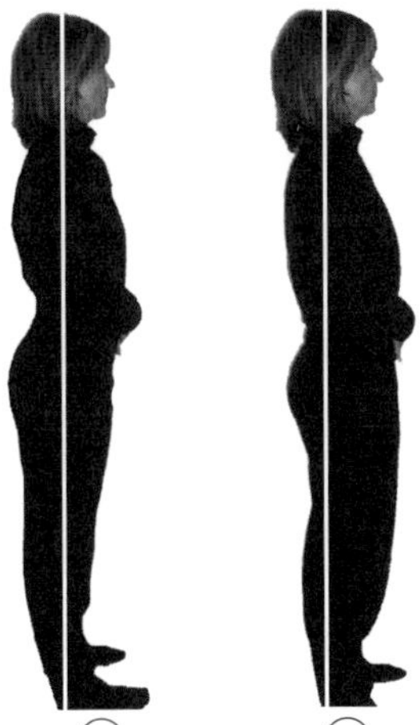

(A) (B)

☐ **Hips and Stomach**
Straighten the lower back to remove tension from the stomach, and to allow access to the abdominal muscles for deep breathing.

Handy Arms

Keeping the hands and arms relaxed at the sides of the body opens the upper chest for good breathing, and enables gesturing.

Have the children stand in their own space, holding both hands tightly in front of the body. In this position, ask them to recite a rhyme. Register the sensation and observe each other.
- How do we look? Awkward? Insecure? Tense?
- How does this position affect the sound of the voice? Does it sound unpleasant? Weak? Tight?

Have the children hold both hands tightly behind the back as they recite a rhyme. Register the sensation and observe each other.
- How do we look?
- How does this position affect the voice?
- How does this position affect our ability to add gestures?

Ask the children to find a better placement for the arms and hands, then to recite a rhyme. Register the sensation and observe each other.
- How do we look?
- What is the difference in the voice when the arms are in a better position?

☐ **Hands and Arms**
Keep the hands and arms relaxed at the sides of the body to open the upper chest for effective breathing, and to enable gesturing.

Chest and Shoulders

To open the chest for good breathing, keep the shoulders relaxed, forming a **T** with the spine.

Have the children stand in their own space. Hold the shoulders up to the ears, and recite a rhyme. The sound will be distorted due to the tension and restriction of the voice.

Drop the shoulders, and repeat the rhyme. The sound will be freer, due to the relaxed position of the shoulders.

☐ **Chest and Shoulders**
Keep the shoulders relaxed, forming a **T** with the spine, to open the chest for breathing.

Ask the children to release their shoulders even more. Often, they haven't completely relaxed their shoulders, so the shoulders will drop another inch or so. Make sure that the shoulders aren't rolled forward, which restricts the chest area, or pulled back, which tightens the muscles across the chest. These positions directly affect the breath as it supports the voice.

The Shoulder Roll

Roll the shoulders to relax further.

Have the children stand in their own space, and roll shoulders forward slowly in a circular motion. Roll shoulders the size of:

- A ping pong ball
- A tennis ball
- A baseball
- A basketball

Repeat the exercise, rolling the shoulders backwards slowly.

Now relax the shoulders. How does this feel? The children will notice how loose their shoulders can be, and how this position opens the throat and frees the area around the vocal folds.

Head and Chinny, Chin, Chin

Tension in the neck affects the vocal folds, thus directly affecting voice quality. Aim to keep the chin parallel to the floor to keep the neck muscles free of tension.

☐ **Head and Chin**
Rest the head on top of the spine, and hold the chin parallel to the floor to free the neck muscles.

Have the children stand in their own space to do this sequence:

- Tuck the chin towards the chest. Count to ten.
- Raise the head to the center. Count to ten again.
- Stretch the chin up and tilt the head back. Count to ten again.

How do these head placements affect the voice? The voice is muffled when the head is tucked down, and strained when the head is pulled back.

Arty in Proper Alignment: A Checklist

- ☐ **Body**
  Stand tall and relaxed, with everything falling into proper alignment.

- ☐ **Head and Chin**
  Rest the head on top of the spine, and hold the chin parallel to the floor to free the neck muscles.

- ☐ **Smile!**

- ☐ **Chest and Shoulders**
  Keep the shoulders relaxed, forming a T with the spine, to open the chest for breathing.

- ☐ **Hands and Arms**
  Keep the hands and arms relaxed at the sides of the body to open the upper chest for effective breathing, and to enable gesturing.

- ☐ **Hips and Stomach**
  Straighten the lower back to remove tension from the stomach, and to allow access to the abdominal muscles for deep breathing.

- ☐ **Knees**
  Keep the knees straight, but not locked.

- ☐ **Feet**
  Stay in balance by keeping the feet slightly apart, and centering the weight on the balls of the feet.

All in Alignment

Often, children are asked to stand as if they were reaching for an object directly above them. However, this causes tension, as they aim to reach up towards the object. To practice proper alignment, do the following exercise:

Unrolling the body and standing properly provides energy and vitality, adding power to the voice.

Stand as if the body were being held by a string connected to the crown of the head, like a marionette. Capture the feeling of dangling from the string. In this position, the entire physical instrument is held loosely, as if suspended in the air.

Add more strings to various body parts, as follows:

- *Right elbow.* Raise the arm from the elbow. Hold. Release and drop the arm to the side. *Register the sensation.*
- *Right wrist.* Raise the arm from the wrist. Hold. Release and drop the arm to the side. *Register the sensation.*
- Continue through other body parts, releasing all tension, and placing the body into a state of relaxation.

Conclude the exercise by imagining that all of the strings have been cut, except for the string attached to the crown of the head. Stand tall and relaxed.

Discuss the effect of standing tall on the way we perceive a person's poise and confidence. Children will likely observe that confident people stand tall and poised, and appear comfortable while looking at the audience. People who lack confidence tend to slouch, avoid eye contact, fidget, and generally look uncomfortable.

Page 29

The illustration of Arty standing in proper alignment demonstrates the desired positioning of the body. Always explain to the children the reasons WHY the body parts need to be held in a certain way, and the impact of body position on voice quality.

Did you know that we are at least an inch taller in the morning than we are at night? This is the effect of slouching, and gravity that pulls the body down through the day.

Top It Off

Did you ever try walking around while balancing a book on your head? The object of this exercise is to walk ever so carefully, with *proper posture*, so the book remains securely in place on the top of the head. I have found that the use of a heavy book tends to result in extra tension in the body. Bodies become rigid in an attempt to hold the book in place, which adds tension in the arms and hands. A book can still be used to reinforce proper alignment; however, I prefer a lighter object, such as a beanbag or a small stuffed animal.

Have everyone place a beanbag on top of the head. Walk easily around the room. Try hard not to let the beanbag fall off!

The presence of an object on the head draws the body upward, and the child walks tall, without added tension.

Notice how the body needs to be positioned to maintain balance, and to keep the beanbag on the head. Ask the children to describe elements of this position, and expect responses such as *standing straight*, *arms are to the sides*, *chin is parallel to the floor*, *eyes are straight ahead*, and so on.

☐ **Smile!**

Encourage the children to relax their faces by *smiling*. Smiling actually releases more tension from the body!

Obstacle Course Challenge

Prepare an obstacle course consisting of chairs, tables, music stands, with objects placed on or beside them. Children will navigate their way through the course, picking up items and placing them around the space as directed.

Have the children place a beanbag on the head, and move easily around the room, avoiding bumping into the obstacles. When they reach a chair, they sit down, then get up again, and move on. When they reach an object, they pick it up, put it down, and move on. Continue through the obstacle course, keeping the beanbag from falling off the head.

Proper alignment facilitates ease of movement.

If the beanbag does fall, be aware of the direction it falls. It will fall because the body is shifting awkwardly in that direction. The body will need to be adjusted to balance the beanbag.

What has to happen to keep the beanbag secure in other positions? When sitting, the children will notice that they need to sit taller. When reaching for an object, the children will need to avoid tilting the head up or down.

The key to good alignment is to adjust the body into a balanced position while moving through the space.

Arty Falls in Line

by Shirley Konrad

Arty had a problem 'cause
He couldn't stand up tall.
His feet were tight together, so
Unbalanced, he would fall.

His teacher tried to help him
Place his feet a foot apart,
But once his feet were in their place
His head to droop did start.

His hands were very awkward
Held so tightly in the back.
This made his breathing difficult,
And power he did lack.

But once he figured out his stance,
Arms loosely at the side,
He stood with strength and confidence —
And spoke with skill and pride.

Playing with Poetry

Introduce the poem ***Arty Falls in Line*** to reinforce the relationship between alignment and proper vocal production.

Page 32

Read the poem once, asking the children to identify places in the poem that suggest actions. Ask them to physically demonstrate the words *unbalanced*, *droop*, *awkward*, *tightly*, *loosely*, and *confidence*.

Read the poem again, this time with the children providing the actions as the words are read. You may need to read the poem several times until the children are familiar with the text.

Consider assigning readers to this poem for use as Readers Theatre. The children can work in small groups or with partners to develop their interpretation and presentation of the script.

Alignment Muscle Memory

Challenge the children to achieve proper alignment as quickly and naturally as they can by doing this exercise.

First, pre-determine a signal, such as a hand clap or verbal cue, which will be used to stop the movement.

Then, ask everyone to move freely around the room. At the sound of the signal, the children are to stop, and confidently position themselves into proper alignment. Check ***Arty in Proper Alignment***, on page 29, to reinforce the elements of proper body positioning.

Children are constantly self-monitoring to find a physical position that is comfortable.

Continue doing this exercise until the children can position themselves without having to *think* about specific placement. Through repetition, the children will give their bodies the opportunity to *memorize* the feeling of proper alignment.

This alignment is the desirable position for standing in front of an audience, and for releasing the voice.

When the body is comfortably aligned, the chest will be open for effective **breathing**. This is the next step to examine to achieve vocal support and power.

Breathing

STEP 3

Proper **breathing** for speech cannot be stressed enough, since breathing is the most important element in voice production. Poor breathing habits limit the potential of the voice, directly affecting *power* and *strength*.

The breathing activities are divided into three main areas of focus:

- Centering the breath
- Increasing the capacity of the breath
- Developing control of the breath

Centering the Breath

The exercises in this section help children to concentrate on centering the breath — that is, using the diaphragm and the abdominal muscles to provide power and support for speaking.

Beginning to Breathe

To begin the exploration of breathing, ask the children to stand in alignment and take a very **deep** breath. Most likely, there will be a dramatic lifting of the shoulders as everyone *sucks in* an audible breath. This simple task clearly demonstrates the most common mistake made during deep inhalation — lifting the shoulders and chest, rather than using the movement of the abdomen and diaphragm for *central breathing*.

The most common mistake made during inhalation for speech is raising the shoulders and chest, rather than using the abdomen and diaphragm.

Have everyone breathe in again, this time asking them to place one hand on the chest, and the other hand on the abdomen and diaphragm (stomach area), keeping arms and shoulders relaxed. Take another deep breath.

- Which area *moved* during inhalation?

If the upper chest or shoulders moved, repeat the inhalation, this time focusing on pulling the breath deeper in towards the stomach muscles.

Did you know that hiccups are produced when the diaphragm sharply contracts? Instead of breathing in normally, the vocal folds shut quickly, producing the *hic* sound.

Direct the children's attention to the movement in the stomach area.

- Did the ribs *stretch* as the lungs filled with air?
- Was there a feeling of expansion into the back?

It is more important to experience the *feeling* of where the breath should be placed than it is to understand the technical process.

Breath Takes Center Stage

It is necessary for expansion to occur in the *stomach* area to produce a strong tone. When *central breathing* is used, there is a greater reserve of air, so phrases can be sustained longer.

Have the children stand in proper alignment. Ask the children to breathe incorrectly by breathing into the upper chest and exaggerating the use of the shoulders.

Exhale while counting aloud as far as possible on one breath.

- How high are they able to count before running out of breath?

To control the pace of the counting, lead the exercise by conducting a beat pattern; otherwise, the children will rush to reach the highest number, defeating the intent of the exercise.

Have the children breathe properly, using the stomach muscles to help draw in as much air as possible. Wait to begin counting until the children feel completely full with the breath.

The breath is deeper and easier to control when *central breathing* is used.

Once again, count aloud as far as possible on one breath.

- What is the difference? Which one is easier?

The children will observe that using central breathing facilitates greater control, and allows them to count much higher.

Laughter

The muscles involved with laughing are also those that are used for central breathing. After the muscles contract, they relax and become stronger. This muscle strength is required for projection.

Ask the children to describe what happens when they laugh.

- How does the stomach feel? Does it bounce?
- What happens when you laugh harder? Does it ache?

Ask the children if there is a difference in the way we laugh in certain situations. For example, some laughter is long, some is deep, some is more like a giggle. How does laughter change in each of the following situations? Try laughing as if:

- Your brother or sister is doing something funny.
- You are watching a clown.
- Someone told a joke, but it isn't *that* funny.
- Something makes you laugh uncontrollably.

Did you know that laughter positively affects your body by making breathing much deeper? Laughter also raises your body temperature, making you feel warmer.

Place both hands on the stomach. **LAUGH!** Feel what happens to the muscles in the stomach area. At first, the laugh may seem forced, but soon the children begin laughing genuinely. The abdominal muscles will bounce up and down. This is the area where inhalation should be concentrated.

The G-i-g-g-l-e C-h-a-i-n

Have the children lie on their backs. Each child places the back of his or her head upon the stomach of the next person, forming a long zig-zagging line. This activity can be done in one large group, or in smaller groups of five or six.

Laughter strengthens the stomach muscles, which are essential to support the voice and assist with the vocal quality produced.

The first person begins a giggle. A domino effect will occur, sending the laughter down the line. Soon the whole class will erupt into laughter.

Ask the children what caused the laughter to become so contagious. They will observe that the movement of another person's stomach bouncing against their heads felt funny , and that laughter was the only possible response!

Doggie Breath

Have the children get down on all fours, like a puppy dog. Ask them to imagine that they have raced around the park chasing a cat, and are panting heavily. *The panting will be quick and energetic.*

Limiting the use of the shoulders focuses the breath into the center of the body.

Contrast this by asking them to try a gentle pant, as if the puppy dog has fallen asleep on his blanket. *The panting will be slower and more gentle.*

The children should feel the movement in the centre of the body, and can experience this by placing one hand on the stomach to feel the connection of the stomach muscles to the breath.

Bouncing Objects

Have the children lie down on the floor, and place either a small book or a small beanbag animal on the stomach. Beanbag animals work very well because they respond to the movement of the body.

Ask the children to breathe in and feel the object rise up effortlessly, as if rising on a balloon as it is inflated. As the air rushes out, the object lowers.

Caution
Objects placed on the stomach muscles should move up and down naturally with the breath. Avoid raising the object by *pushing* the stomach muscles.

Often, children will force the object up without actually drawing in the air. This movement is quick and tense. The object should rise easily and smoothly with the breath, rather than being pushed up intentionally by the stomach muscles. Draw attention to this difference, and encourage them to feel the connection with the breath.

Increase the inhalation and the exhalation, to imitate a dog panting. The object will bounce up and down, causing spontaneous laughter.

Breathing in the Classroom

Children can center the breath while sitting at their desks.

Ask the children to place their hands as far as possible under their chair and to hold firmly onto the chair. This position prevents the shoulders from moving up and down, so the focus moves to the center of the body.

Have the children breathe as deeply as possible. They will notice expansion in the abdomen, the area used for central breathing.

The Inner Tube Tire

Ask the children to imagine that they have an inner tube tire placed around the waist. It is important to encourage expansion for the breath all the way around the body — front, sides, and back. As they inhale, encourage them to fill up the space, pushing into the inner tube all the way around.

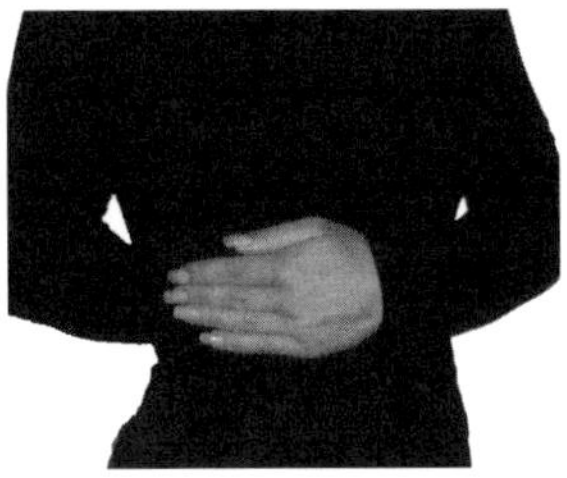

Place one arm around the stomach, and the other arm across the back, keeping the shoulders and arms as relaxed as possible. See photo. Once again, breathe deeply, pressing the breath into the arms.

Remind the children that this is the desired movement when they are asked to *"take a breath."*

Rag Doll Breathing

This exercise focuses on relaxing and opening the lower back with the breath to increase expansion of the central area.

Have the children flop over, like a rag doll held at the waist. Keeping knees slightly bent, and head and neck completely relaxed, have the children hug themselves. Breathe deeply. Feel the air go into the back.

Place the children into pairs, with one child being **A** and the other **B**. **A** flops over from the waist like a rag doll, and **B** stands directly behind. **B** places the palm of the hands on the lower portion of **A**'s back. Encourage the **A**s to breathe deeply, so that the **B**s can feel the breath expanding the lower back. Keep breathing until the **A**s can place the breath easily into this region.

Did you know that two-thirds of the lungs are located in the back of the body, not in the front? That is why the doctor listens to your breathing by placing a stethoscope on your back.

A continues breathing in this manner, while rolling up the spine to stand in proper alignment. Breathing should be centered.

Repeat the exercise, with the **B**s doing the breathing.

Moving with the Breath

Often, children breathe well until it comes time for the actual performance. The performance situation creates nervousness, which causes them to hold their voices in, limiting the use of the breath.

Use jumping jacks as a quick exercise to encourage energetic and deep breathing.

When I hear a child begin to speak with a voice that is unusually weak and obviously lacking breath support, I ask him or her to quickly do ten jumping jacks. I count aloud, using an energetic voice to stimulate the energy exerted for the jumping jacks. This is a quick way to remind the children to breathe.

As soon as the child stops, I ask him or her to speak again. *Voila!* The voice is now more connected to the breath, and is full and rich.

When the breath is centered, and support is provided by the muscles of exhalation, the amount of air expelled can increase significantly. This can be achieved through exercises focusing on **increasing the capacity of the breath**.

Increasing the Capacity of the Breath

The exercises in this section focus on developing the muscles required for increasing the capacity of the breath to support the voice. Choppy reading, the result of taking frequent breaths, can be avoided when the breath supply is increased.

The S l o o o o o w Leak

For this activity, you will need a stop watch, or a clock with a second hand.

Have the children stand in good alignment, and take a deep breath without raising the shoulders. Time them as they release the air with a **sssss** sound, as if they have developed a slow leak.

- If a child can last only about ten seconds, it is a sure sign that the abdomen and diaphragm are not being used properly.
- Encourage the children to make the **sssss** sound last for at least 15 to 20 seconds.

Did you know that we breathe 10 to 14 times per minute? Each day, we take in about 500 cubic feet of air; in a lifetime, we will breathe nearly 14,000,000 cubic feet of air — enough to fill an oil tanker!

Remind the children not to force the air out abruptly, but to keep the sound smooth and controlled, like a *s l o o o o o w* leak. The sound does not need to be very loud.

Alphabet & Number Race

Another way to increase breath capacity is with this quick exercise.

Say the alphabet on one breath. Ensure that the children speak slowly and clearly. Now try to go through the alphabet *twice* on one breath.

Repeat the exercise, this time with numbers, speaking as far as possible on one breath. Check to make sure that the children don't release too much air on the numbers that start with **s**, **th**, or **f**.

Children can challenge themselves to increase breath capacity.

Challenge the children to exceed their *personal best* each time they do this exercise.

The Breathing Maze

In this exercise, children are asked to apply their skill of increased breath capacity to a game.

Page 125

Reproduce the maze diagram on page 125, providing one copy for each child.

Arty has lost his marbles, and must find all the marbles by going through the maze. The object of this exercise is to travel from one marble to the next on a single breath.

The child starts off with a finger on Arty, and uses it as a guide to travel through the maze. Ask the child to breathe out on a continuous **sss** or **zzz** sound while moving through the maze. The child may stop to take a fresh breath *only* at each lost marble, but not in between. If a breath is taken in between marbles, the child must go back to the last marble. Remind the child to control the sound with an even flow of air, rather than expelling all of the air at the beginning, and quickly running out of breath.

Through games, children can apply and practice new knowledge of breathing.

How many breaths does the child need to get through the maze? It should be possible to complete the maze on nine breaths. *Notice that, the faster the finger moves through the maze, the less effective this exercise is for strengthening necessary muscles.*

Encourage the children to go *very slowly* so that they have to use the abdominal muscles to drive the air out and to control the **sss** or **zzz** sound. Placing one hand on the stomach is a reminder to the child that the movement for exhalation needs to come from the central region of the body. See photo. Focusing the movement for exhalation in this area is called the *abdominal press.*

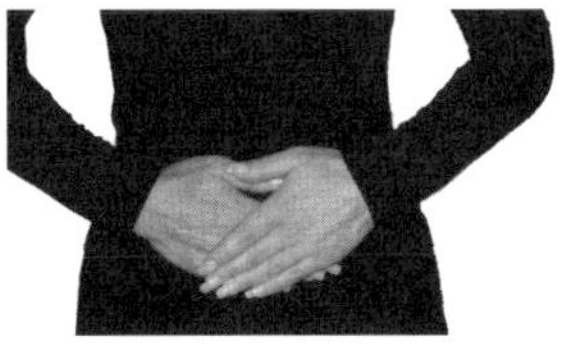

Challenge the children to see who can release sound and breath the *most slowly* from marble to marble.

School's Begun

by Marilyn Smith

Reader 1	1 one,
Reader 2	School's begun.
Reader 3	2 two,
Reader 4	What shall we do?
Reader 2	3 three,
Reader 3	Read to me!
Reader 1	4 four,
Reader 4	Stories galore.
Reader 3	5 five,
Reader 4	Peek inside.
Reader 1	6 six,
Reader 2	Can I pick?
Reader 4	7 seven,
Reader 3	Love to listen.
Reader 2	8 eight,
Reader 1	Just can't wait.
Reader 3	9 nine,
Reader 4	Stories are fine.
Reader 1	10 ten,
ALL	Read it again!

Playing with Poetry

Introduce the poem ***School's Begun***, by Marilyn Smith. Have everyone read it together several times.

Page 40

When the children are comfortable with the text, take in a single breath to speak the first stanza, then stop and release any remaining breath.

> 1 one,
> School's begun. b

Start again at the beginning of the poem, this time going to the end of the second stanza on a single breath.

Practicing leads to the use of centered and controlled breathing.

> 1 one,
> School's begun.
>
> 2 two,
> What shall we do? b

Continue speaking the text in this way until the children can say the whole poem on one breath! The more the abdominal muscles are exercised, the stronger and more supported the voice becomes.

Perform the poem using cumulative voices. Begin with one voice for the first stanza. Add an extra voice with each stanza so that there are ten voices speaking on the last stanza. This can also be done using groups of voices, rather than single voices, to build the sound.

Encourage the children to use as few breaths as possible as they build the voices through the poem. Mark the scripts with places to breathe, so that they aim to achieve the effect of a unified voice.

Page 121

Any sequence poem will work for this exercise.

- ***Summer's Done***, **Early Literacy — A Seasonal Approach**
- ***Countdown to Christmas***, **Invitation to Readers Theatre**
- ***One, Two, Buckle My Shoe***, Nursery Rhyme

> With increased capacity of the breath, it is necesary to **control the outgoing breath** and discover its relationship to volume.

Developing Control of the Breath

To further increase the strength of the muscles related to breathing and volume, work on control with the following exercise.

The Volume Button

Have the children stand in proper alignment, placing the hands on the stomach.

- Count from 1 to 10, increasing volume as the numbers increase, reaching the strongest volume at 10.

Focus on the stomach muscles to develop an understanding of their role in increasing and decreasing volume.

Remind the children that a *big voice* is not the same as *shouting*. Shouting is straining from the throat, and must be avoided. Avoid raising the pitch level as the voice increases in volume. This is a sure sign that the voice is being pushed from the throat, rather than being supported by the abdominal muscles.

Volume, page 113

- Decrease volume while counting backwards from 10, reaching the softest volume at 1.

Expand this activity by reciting one stanza from a familiar nursery rhyme, such as ***Jack and Jill***.

Symbols, page 77

Begin by saying the rhyme softly. Gradually increase the volume through the first section.

Jack and Jill went up the hill to fetch a pail of water.

Decrease the volume to a soft voice by the end of the rhyme.

Jack fell down and broke his crown and Jill came tumbling after.

Practice reciting the rhyme until it can be spoken comfortably on one breath.

> When the exhaled air is centered, controlled, and has increased capacity, it is ready to be converted into strong sound waves through the process of **phonation**.

Phonation

STEP 4

All of the air that enters and leaves the lungs passes through the *larynx*, or *voice box*. It is on the exhaled breath that sound is produced. This process is called **phonation**.

Have the children experiment with the breath:

- Breathe in while saying your full name.
- Breathe out while saying your full name.

What happens? This experiment shows that it is on the *outgoing* breath that sound is produced properly.

The Voice Box and the Vocal Folds

The *larynx* is the basis for the human voice. Inside the larynx, or *voice box*, are *vocal folds*. The term *folds* clearly identifies their operation, because the action is that of the muscles *folding* back and forth. In normal breathing, the vocal folds move apart to allow air to flow freely between them. To enable speaking, the vocal folds come together, and air rushing over their edges produces sound.

Did you know that the vocal folds vibrate approximately 256 times per second at middle C?

Although called the *voice box*, the larynx is, in fact, a type of tubular box that *houses* the vocal folds. You can feel the front of the larynx by placing your fingers gently on your throat, just under the chin. Feel the thick cartilage that protects the vocal folds. This is also known as the *Adam's Apple*.

Did you know that, according to folklore, when Adam bit into the apple in the Garden of Eden, it got stuck in his throat, and he choked a bit? Hence, the term *Adam's Apple*.

Because of the name, it is easy to imagine the vocal folds to be like *cords* or *strings*. Actually, they are two sheets of muscles with a small triangular gap between them. This gap is called the *glottis*. These folds move together, producing a slit through which the air passes, resulting in sound.

Sound is affected by both the *tension* and *length* of the vocal folds.

- Tighter and shorter folds produce a higher pitch.
- Longer and looser folds produce a lower pitch.

Understanding the role the vocal folds play in voice production

Playing with Sound

Show the children a balloon, and ask them to imagine that it represents their lungs. The neck of the balloon is similar to the throat.

Blow a small amount of air into the balloon. Hold the neck of the balloon between your finger and thumb. Let the air rush out.

In the same way that less air in the balloon produces a weak sound, while a lot of air produces a stronger sound, less air in the lungs produces a weaker voice, while a greater supply of air supports a stronger voice.

Blow even more air into the balloon, and let the neck of the balloon go again. Notice what happens. What is the difference?

Holding the neck of the balloon with both hands, stretch the opening of the balloon from side to side so that it makes a narrow slit, like the vocal folds. Let the air rush out. Notice what happens. As the air comes through the slit, it makes a *squealing* sound. The longer the slit, the higher the pitch, and the shorter the slit, the lower the pitch.

Activating the Adam's Apple

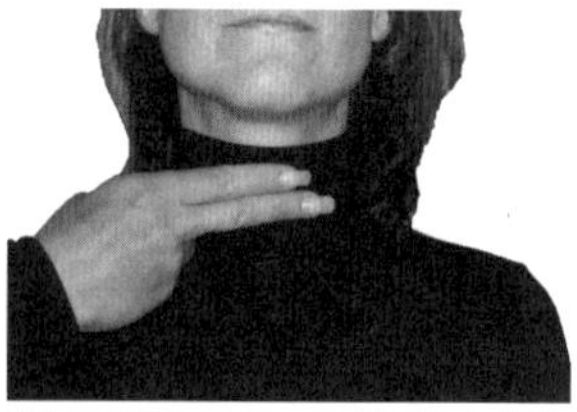

Place fingers gently on throat to feel vocal cord vibrations.

Yawn to relax the throat muscles. Encourage the children to keep the chin level with the floor, which keeps the neck free of tension.

Say **awww** (as in *ball*). While saying this sound, gently place two fingers on the middle of the throat where the vibration is occurring. See photo. What does it feel like?

Say a different sound, such as **ooo** (as in *boot*) or **eee** (as in *beet*). Is there a difference? Check to determine whether the sounds are voiced or voiceless by feeling for the vibrations against the fingers. You will notice that all vowel sounds are *voiced*; that is, produced with vocal fold vibration.

Caution: Take care with the way the sound is made. Saying the *name* of the letter adds a vowel sound (**tee**).

However, not all sounds are voiced. The consonants **f**, **h**, **k**, **p**, **s**, **sh**, **t**, **th** (as in three), and **wh** are all *voiceless*. These voiceless sounds are shaped by the way the air escapes and the way the articulators fit together.

Things U-Otter-Know about Throat Care

According to a study done by throat specialists at the University of California, gargling is one of the worst things to do for a sore throat. Throat clearing doesn't help either. Instead, drink plenty of water to keep the throat moist. Both teachers and students can benefit from using personal water bottles when doing vocal work.

Yawning Arty

by Shirley Konrad

Arty got up in the morning
As tired as he could be.
He y a w n e d when he slipped off the covers,
And y a w n e d as he slurped his tea.

He y a w n e d as he crawled to the bathroom,
He y a w n e d as he scrubbed his hair,
He y a w n e d as he chewed his toothbrush,
Because he wasn't quite there.

He y a w n e d and he y a w n e d and he y a w n e d,
And then he y a w n e d some more.
Then Arty curled up in his blanket,
And slept peacefully on the floor.

Playing with Poetry

Yawning prepares children for performance by opening and relaxing the throat.

Page 45

Introduce the poem ***Yawning Arty*** by first discussing yawning.

- When do we yawn? Why do we yawn?
- **YAWN!** How does a yawn make you feel? Tired? Relaxed?

Encourage the children to *sigh* audibly at the end of the yawn, because stifling the sigh creates tension in the throat muscles. Notice the sound that is produced — this is the most open and relaxed sound that can be created.

Caution: Don't do this if you are really tired, unless you are prepared to have the entire class fall asleep on you!

Read ***Yawning Arty*** aloud. In this poem, Arty is *sooooo* tired that he yawns all the way through his morning ritual. As you say the word *yawned*, attach a yawn to your delivery so the word is stretched out. Notice that the children will begin yawning with you as well!

Say the poem together. As the poem is read, encourage the children to stretch the mouth widely, adding a yawning quality to the word *yawned*. Most will produce real yawns, with open throats.

Is yawning contagious? Although some sources attribute yawning to a need for oxygen, and a way to get rid of extra carbon monoxide in the body, most sources agree that it is a mysterious subject, and that simply the *thought* of yawning can produce the reaction.

A common belief is that yawning is psychological, because you can tell yourself not to do it, and you won't. This is probably why it is not contagious. Try *thinking* your way out of a yawn the next time you see someone open his or her mouth wide as a reaction to fatigue or boredom.

Read the poem together again. Encourage physical involvement:

- Use the arms to stretch while yawning. This will help to relax the body.
- At the end of the poem, lie on the floor, imitating a relaxed Arty. How does the body feel? Is it stiff? Relaxed? Is it heavy? Light?

Remind the children that this is what they want to feel prior to any performance — a relaxed body and relaxed throat, free of unnecessary tension. Tight throat muscles create a high, strained voice, so it is important to remember to relax the throat muscles. Yawning is one of the best ways to relax the throat.

> When the sound is open and relaxed in the throat, it is ready to be amplified by the resonating cavities in order to achieve richness in the quality produced. **Resonance** is the next step in effective voice production.

Resonance

STEP 5

Once the breath becomes a vibrating column of air through the process of phonation, it travels up and **resonates** in the *main cavities* of the *throat*, *mouth*, and *nose*. Very deep sounds resonate in the *chest*, while very high sounds resonate in the *sinuses*. Sounds travelling through all the cavities are reinforced and amplified, directly affecting the quality of the sound.

The Throat Cavity

A *tight* throat produces a voice quality that is harsh and strident. An *open* throat produces a fuller, richer voice. Yawning exercises relax the throat.

Yawning, page 46

Isolating the Throat Cavity

Sound resonates in the throat cavity when it is open and relaxed.

Ask the children to stand comfortably in proper alignment. Ensure that shoulders are relaxed. Have them raise the arms and place hands and fingers gently around the throat. Aim the voice towards the back of the mouth and into the throat, and say **awww** (as in *ball*). Feel the vibration in the throat cavity.

Say the nursery rhyme ***Mary Had a Little Lamb***, keeping the vibration in the throat, rather than in the mouth and nose. Observe the quality of the voice. If the vibration is kept only in the throat, the pitch will remain low.

The Oral Cavity

The oral cavity is the largest and most flexible of the resonators. The articulators — *lips*, *teeth*, *tongue*, *hard palate*, *soft palate*, and *jaw* — are located here. The articulators improve the quality of sounds produced, allowing them to be clear and distinct.

Isolating the Oral Cavity

Sound also resonates in the oral cavity.

Stand comfortably in proper alignment. Encourage the children to blow air into the cheeks, placing the focus on the mouth, rather than on the throat. Release the air. Now place the fingers gently on the cheeks and say **ee** (as in *beet*). Keep the lips stretched wide. Feel the vibration on the fingertips as you aim the voice toward the front of the cheeks.

Say the nursery rhyme ***Mary Had a Little Lamb***, keeping the vibration in the mouth rather than in the throat and nose. If the children are struggling, encourage them to put more energy into the lip action, which will help pull the sound more forward.

Explore resonance in the throat and oral cavities.

Enhance Resonance

Resonance improves, and is better controlled, after exploring the effect the throat and oral cavities have on vocal quality.

Have the children stand comfortably in proper alignment. Initiate a big yawn to ensure the throat is open and relaxed. Sigh audibly at the end of the yawn.

Tilt the head back slightly, leaving the mouth open wide, and the jaw relaxed. Let out a long **awww** (as in *ball*) sound. Increased vibrations should be felt in the mouth and throat cavities.

Roll the head to the side while letting out a long **awww**. Roll the head towards the chest while letting out another long **awww**. Listen to the changes in voice quality as the head moves to different positions.

Raise the head to a neutral position. Pinch the nose and say **awww**. The sound should stay in the mouth. Eliminate any placement of this sound in the nose. Alternate opening and closing the nostrils while saying **awww**, keeping the sound in the mouth.

Say the following sentences, which contain no nasal sounds, keeping the focus in the mouth and throat:

- Play outside with the other kids.
- Betty the baker baked big cookies.
- While you wait, whistle for a while.

The Nasal Cavity

Soft Palate, page 56

The nasal cavity is responsible for the **m**, **n**, and **ng** sounds. All other sounds travel through the oral cavity. To produce these nasal sounds, the soft palatc rclaxcs, allowing air to travel through the nasal passage.

Sound can resonate in the nasal cavity.

Isolating the Nasal Cavity

Stand comfortably in proper alignment. Change the focus away from the mouth and throat by gently massaging the nose.

Aim the voice toward the nose, and hold a long **mmmmm** while placing the fingertips gently on either side of the nose. Feel the vibrations in this area. The soft palate relaxes, letting the sound travel into the nose.

Say the nursery rhyme ***Mary Had a Little Lamb***, keeping the vibration in the nose. If the nasal sounds are not resonated in the nasal cavity, the voice will sound as if the child has a cold.

Don't Close the Nose!

Use these as quick warm-ups prior to a speech performance or Readers Theatre presentation.

Explore humming to open the nasal cavity.

Have the children stand comfortably in proper alignment.

Hum! Breathe deeply to ensure good breath control. Hum playfully. Continue humming while gently massaging all parts of the face. This action opens the cavities further, and strengthens response to the sound.

Chew! Exaggerate the muscles in the face and mouth, and pretend to chew, while humming with a closed mouth. The sound will be muffled. Move the chew around to loosen the face by directing the hum into different areas of the face — ***cheeks***, ***lips***, ***forehead***, and ***nose***.

Stretch! Attach the hum to an imaginary thread, and stretch it to various objects around the room. This brings the focus to the lips, and draws the sound forward.

Slide! Imagine the hum going *down* a slide. Begin at the top of the slide, and go all the way down! Keep the sound directed into the nose, and keep fingers on either side of the nose to feel the vibration. Reverse the direction of the hum, going *up* the slide. This action continues to open up the nasal cavity while playing with pitch.

Say **mmmmm** as if:

- You have just eaten your favorite dessert (a *yummy* **mmm**)
- Thinking aloud (a *wondering* **mmm**)
- Agreeing with your friend (a *positive* **mmm**)
- Doubting a story your friend just told you (a *suspicious* **mmm**)

Repeat the above exercise, this time adding vowels to the hum:

- **M**ah, **m**ay, **m**oh, **m**oo, **m**igh

Repeat the exercise, using the **n** sound:

- **N**ah, **n**ay, **n**oh, **n**oo, **n**igh

Resonance is increased in the nasal cavity when the sounds **m**, **n**, and **ng** are placed properly.

Say the following phrases, concentrating on the nasal sounds **m**, **n**, and **ng**:

- A lo**ng**, lo**ng** trai**n**
- Rhy**ming** sig**n**s
- Shi**n**i**ng** su**n**
- Rai**n** i**n** Spai**n**
- Ti**m**e a**n**d ti**m**e a**n**d ti**m**e agai**n**

The Chest and Sinus Cavities

Extreme pitches are resonated in the chest and sinus cavities.

The ***chest*** reinforces the very low tones in the voice. Imagine the voice of a giant — it would be low and deep.

The ***sinuses*** reinforce the very high tones. Imagine the high-pitched voices of the pigs in ***The Three Little Pigs***.

Looney *Tones*

Developing voices for characters encourages children to explore the qualities of different personalities, and allows them to explore their own vocal range. Using character voices affords the opportunity to explore the extreme pitches that resonate in the chest and sinus cavities.

Children can explore their own vocal range by playing with character voices.

Bring an assortment of cartoon strips to the class. Have the children read the cartoon strips, using different voices for each character.

Invite the children to explain why they have chosen the kind of voice they have for each of the characters. Cartoon character voices are created by interfering with the resonators, and tightening the muscles of the mouth and throat.

This discussion will likely involve an explanation of *stereotypes*. For example, we associate large characters with deep, rumbly voices, and small characters with high-pitched voices.

Balanced Resonance

It is important to balance the primary resonators — ***throat***, ***mouth***, and ***nose*** — to achieve a rich vocal quality. Remember that nasal sounds are amplified primarily by the nasal cavities, while the vowel sounds are resonated in the throat and mouth.

When the sound is reinforced by the cavity resonators, it is ready to be shaped by the articulators, or the parts of the mouth responsible for clear and distinct speech. **Articulation** is explored as the next vital step in producing the voice.

Articulation

> A new student of mine mentioned that she liked a book called **The Alice**. I was confused, and repeated, *"**The Alice**?"* She replied, *"No, **The Alice**!"* I probed further, only to discover that she was not saying **The Alice**, but **The Atlas**! Without the clear **t** sound, the word changed completely. The need for clarity in speech is self-evident.

STEP 6

Articulation focuses on adjusting and managing the parts of the mouth that shape consonant sounds and promote clarity. The articulators include the *lips*, *teeth*, *tongue*, *hard palate*, *soft palate*, and *jaw*.

Improvements in articulation can be made from a very early age. However, the longer a habit remains unchecked, the more work it takes to correct. Teachers play a significant role in modeling, correcting, and guiding children to become clear and articulate speakers.

Because of its collaborative nature, Readers Theatre is an excellent vehicle for developing proper speech habits that children can easily integrate into daily speaking. Working with a group of children takes the focus away from an individual, and provides a secure and comfortable working environment for a child who may be self-conscious about an articulation problem.

The collaborative nature of Readers Theatre supports exploration of vocal expression and strengthens confidence levels.

The importance of repetition and practice cannot be overemphasized. Practice prior to performance should always include warm-ups such as tongue twisters, which promote flexible articulators.

Tongue Twisters, page 58

Articulation Difficulties

When a child is not easily understood, it may be a sign that articulation difficulties require attention and correction. Articulation delays or disorders are defined as errors in a child's production of consonant sounds that do not appear to be consistent with the child's chronological age.

There are general developmental stages that children go through in the acquisition of normal speech and articulation. Occasionally, there may be speech difficulties apart from these stages that are considered *outside of the norm*. For example, by kindergarten, a child should have no difficulty in the production of consonant sounds, with the exception of the **l**, **r**, **s**, **z**, and **th** sounds. These are typically the last sounds to be developed, usually by the age of seven or eight.

Early detection and intervention are important when a teacher suspects that a child is exhibiting articulation difficulties.

A teacher is often the first to notice a child experiencing voice difficulties. The teacher may observe that the child's voice appears to differ significantly from what would be expected to be *normal* quality, for example, pitch or volume, in relation to the child's age, gender, and physical size. The child's voice quality will often be described as *unpleasant*, *hoarse*, *monotonal*, or *too nasal*, *too low*, or *too loud*.

However, a teacher can address minor articulation problems in the classroom. For example, children often substitute the w sound for an **r** sound. In this case, the child would say, *"The wabbit wan awound the wock,"* instead of *"The rabbit ran around the rock."* Use the information below to help children overcome this common problem.

Things U-Otter-Know about the Sound R

To make a clear **r** (errr) sound, encourage the children to bring the tip of the tongue close to the gum ridge, and turn it back slightly toward the middle of the hard palate, which is the arched roof of the mouth.

It is important to emphasize the movement of the front part of the tongue. The lips must be energized and pulled forward to help shape the sound further. If the child is keeping the tongue flat or immobile in the mouth, or raising the back portion of the tongue toward the soft palate, a **w** sound is more likely to be produced.

A-Maze-ing!

The ***Breathing Maze*** activity, described on page 39, is designed to bring attention to and practice the differences in the consonant sounds, promoting good articulation in a fun and supportive manner.

Page 125

The object of this activity is to help Arty find his bag of marbles.

With a finger, follow the maze along while producing the **r** (errr) sound correctly. This activity can be repeated, using any other continuous sound, such as **s**, **z** or **th**.

Consonant Sounds, page 16

Remember that the plosive sounds **b**, **p**, **d**, **t**, **g**, and **k** cannot be used for this exercise, since the flow of air is stopped to produce the sound.

Hissssssssing Sibilants

Until the sibilant **s** and **z** sounds are developed, a word like *sleep* may sound like *thleep*. To encourage correct placement of the tongue tip, have the children say:

The six thick swamp sticks

If the tongue slips out between the teeth, a **th** sound is produced. Place the tip of the tongue lightly behind the top teeth to produce the **s** sound correctly.

Emphasize proper tongue placement, and the importance of exercising the tip of the tongue.

Sometimes, children cannot hear or feel the difference in tongue placement. When this happens, a mirror becomes a valuable tool. Look into a mirror, and say:

Six sticky suckers

Observe the tongue to see whether it comes out between the teeth (**th** sound), or is hidden behind the top teeth (**s** sound).

Continue working with these types of phrases, and reinforce proper tongue placement for the formation of these sibilants.

Did you know that, by age eight, 90% of children are clearly producing the **s** and **z** sounds?

The Art of Articulation

> **"A loud voice cannot compete with a clear voice, even if it's a whisper." — Barry Neil Kaufman**

A *visual* approach to articulation is one of the best ways to introduce this concept. Arty, the puppet on the front cover, was designed specifically for this reason. Arty's articulators are greatly exaggerated, which helps children identify the parts of their own mouth. However, pictures and mirrors also provide assistance for pointing out the articulators.

Tips for the Lips

Understanding the function of the lips

Ask the children to identify the parts of the mouth that are used for shaping speech sounds. Expect a variety of responses, including *the throat*, or *the thing at the back of the mouth.*

To help them understand the specific parts of the mouth used to form consonant sounds, have them say **purple** and **bubble**. After each word, determine which parts of the mouth they used to produce the sounds. The children will notice that the *lips* are active in making the **p** sounds in *purple*, and the **b** sounds in *bubble*. What other consonant sounds need the lips?

Flash cards are a quick tool tor use in pairs or small groups.

To practice lip flexibility, create a set of flash cards, using the consonant sounds found in medial and final positions in ***Humpty Dumpty***.

Have the children recite ***Humpty Dumpty*** together, to make sure that everyone is familiar with the text. Encourage the children to pay attention to *how* the parts of the mouth work together to produce each sound. Now ask them to recite it again, this time WITHOUT moving the lips. This is difficult to do, and it will sound funny. The children will realize how essential the lips are when speaking to be understood!

Expand this activity by checking the formation of other consonant sounds. Have the children say **giggle** and **little**. Which parts of the mouth are active on these sounds? They will notice that the *back of the tongue* is used for the **g** sounds in *giggle*, and the *tongue tip* is used for the **l** and **t** sounds in *little*.

Meet the Teeth

Understanding the function of the teeth

Without the *teeth*, words are muffled and unclear. This exercise helps children become more aware of the function of the teeth in speaking clearly. They will hear and feel the difference between inadequate and adequate sounds.

Have the children say: **Three very fine fresh fish**. What part of the mouth is doing all the work? They may notice that the teeth are especially active in shaping the sounds **f**, **v**, and **th**.

Now ask them to cover their teeth with their lips, as if they have no teeth, and then recite ***Humpty Dumpty***. What happens? They will notice that the sound is muffled and distorted.

Losing the front teeth affects the clarity of sounds, specifically the sibilants **s** and **z**.

Children who lose their front teeth will speak with a bit of a lisp, because their tongues slip out into the empty space normally filled with teeth. The **s** sounds will come out like the sound **th**. This problem usually disappears once the adult teeth grow in.

Jabber Jaw

Understanding the function of the jaw

Overall, Canadians have a tendency to keep the jaw fairly tight while speaking. If you have ever watched comedians imitate Canadians, you may have noticed that they exaggerate the jaw's tenseness, creating a rigid, tight speech pattern.

When the jaw is tight, the opening of the mouth becomes restricted, and the sound is lost inside the mouth, or is placed into the throat. For clear speech, relax the jaw to enable the sound to be released freely. When the jaw is relaxed, more sound is able to escape from the mouth.

Caution!
Never encourage a child to warm up the jaw by moving it from side to side. The jaw is created like a hinge, so the natural movement is up-and-down. Side-to-side movement is actually abusive and unnatural.

To create greater awareness of the mobility of the jaw, and the feeling of a *relaxed* jaw, have the children place a flattened hand two inches below the jaw. Say **yaw**, **yaw**, **yaw**, trying to touch the jaw to the hand. Encourage the children to drop the jaw comfortably, rather than forcing it down. The **yaw** should sound lazy. The children will notice how far the jaw can drop. In fact, the jaw should drop far enough to fit two fingers, one on top of the other, between the teeth.

Chinese Fortune Teller Exercise

Page 126

Using a manipulative tool helps children visualize the actions of the mouth. A Chinese Fortune Teller is quick to make, and works well to illustrate these movements. Instructions are included on page 126 of this guidebook.

Holding the Chinese Fortune Teller in front, open it up and down while saying **ah** (as in *bat*). The jaw will drop far down, releasing the **ah** sound. Manipulate the Fortune Teller to imitate the actions of the mouth; both should be opened wide.

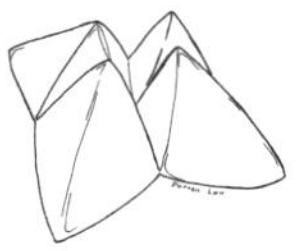

Close the Fortune Teller, saying **oo** (as in *boot*). Encourage the children to round the lips as much as possible. Again, imitate the closed, rounded shape of the mouth with the Fortune Teller.

Open the Fortune Teller in a side-to-side direction, while saying **ee** (as in *beet*). Encourage the children to stretch the lips as widely as possible.

Close the Fortune Teller back to centre, saying **oo** again.

Continue, repeating **ah** — **oo** — **ee** — **oo**, **ah** — **oo** — **ee** — **oo**.

Stretching the mouth into the various positions allows for more mobility, which assists in creating greater clarity of speech.

The Soft Palate

Understanding the function of the soft palate

It is never too early to learn about the soft palate. Have the children use their tongues to explore the roof of the mouth. They will feel that the roof at the top of the mouth is hard against the tongue. This is the *hard palate*. Reaching farther back into the mouth, they will discover a soft part, right above the uvula. This is the *soft palate*.

All speech sounds are produced orally. The breath escapes through the mouth and is shaped by the articulators, with the exception of three sounds — **m**, **n**, and **ng**. These three are called *nasal sounds* because the air escapes through the nasal cavity.

The soft palate controls whether the breath goes into the oral cavity or into the nasal cavity. Too much air going into the nose produces a voice defined as *nasal*. If too little or no air goes into the nose for the nasal sounds, the voice is defined as *denasal*, sounding as if the person has a cold. If there is a concern about whether or not a child has a long-term vocal difficulty related to nasality, consult a Speech-Language Pathologist.

Things U-Otter-Know about the Uvula

- The thing that dangles at the back of the mouth is called the *uvula*. Children often refer to it as the *punching bag*, or mistake it for the tonsils.
- The uvula moves with the soft muscle attached to it, which is called the *soft palate*.
- The uvula serves no obvious purpose, although it may contribute to the vibrations produced while snoring.

A *Nosey* Experiment

Ask the children to hold the nose closed with their fingers, and then repeat the following sounds (not the letter names):

Remind students to produce a pure sound by avoiding vowel addition; that is, say **t**, not **tee**.

s — t — k — b — l — m

Observe where the air is coming out. Is the sound coming out of the mouth (oral cavity) or the nose (nasal cavity)?

Children will notice that the **m** feels different from the other sounds. They will feel blocked, and unable to produce the sound as clearly as they produced the others.

Repeat the exercise, substituting **n** and **ng** for the **m**, to observe the sound placement in the nasal cavity.

Tongue Fun

The **tongue** is the most flexible and most important articulator. We often take the tongue for granted; however, it is the most mobile of the articulators, and deserves the greatest focus.

Understanding the function of the tongue

Things U-Otter-Know about the Tongue

- Did you know that there are three nerves in the tongue? The *gustatory* nerve provides the sensation of taste, the *hypoglossal* nerve allows for movement, and the *pharyngeal* nerve assists in swallowing.
- Did you know that two-thirds of the tongue is free to travel around in the mouth?
- Did you know that the bulk of the tongue is composed of bundles of striped muscle fibre, which enable it to change shape?

Tongue-nastics

Playing with the tongue increases understanding that the tongue is a large muscle that is flexible and easily manipulated. Repeating *tongue-nastics* actually strengthens the tongue and improves flexibility, which leads to better articulation.

Guide the children through the following amazing feats:

- Can you stick out your tongue so far that it touches the tip of your nose? Only one in about a thousand people can perform this amazing trick!
- Can you touch your tongue to your ear? Of course this is impossible, but it does help stretch the sides of the tongue, and assists in eliminating extra tension.
- Can you turn up the sides of your tongue to form a tunnel? This is an inherited trait found in only seven out of ten people.
- Can you turn your tongue into a clover leaf shape? Only one in several thousand people can do this!

Did you know that, even though ventriloquists can produce speech without moving their lips, they can't do it without moving their tongues? Try it!

Encourage the children to exercise the tongue tip to increase the overall muscularity of the tongue, and assist with producing sounds such as **d** and **t**.

Exercising the tongue increases its strength and flexibility.

Focus on the tongue tip by miming the following actions:

- Lick an ice cream cone
- Lick stamps
- Catch snowflakes on the tongue

Tongue Twisters

Peter Piper picked a peck of pickled peppers.
A peck of pickled peppers Peter Piper picked.
If Peter Piper picked a peck of pickled peppers,
Where's the peck of pickled peppers Peter Piper picked?

A version of this well-known tongue twister first appeared in 1813, in a book by J. Harris entitled **Peter Piper's Practical Principles of Plain and Perfect Pronunciation**. Can you say that five times? This book led to the development of numerous exercises using alliteration as a means for training children to speak properly.

However, this twister is probably the most incorrectly spoken by children. Most children are slightly familiar with the first two lines, but when asked to speak the twister slowly, they reveal great confusion with the words. What purpose does saying the tongue twister serve, if the words cannot be understood?

Tongue twisters improve oral skills and strengthen word recognition.

The primary benefit of a tongue twister is to encourage the articulators to move rapidly between sounds, while producing clear and intelligible words. Although it is fun to repeat the phrase at breakneck speed before *tripping up*, the words should never become muddled. Children who cannot say ***Peter Piper*** correctly may not ever have heard it pronounced clearly or accurately.

Introducing Tongue Twisters

Working with tongue twisters is an excellent way to warm up all of the articulators, but most importantly, the tongue. A tongue twister needs to be repeated over and over to adequately challenge the articulators.

Tongue twisters are a series of words that are difficult to say because of their close sequence of similar sounds. For example:

- Black bugs' blood
- Pass the purple pencil, please.
- Ruth's tooth is loose.

Did you know that tongue twisters were originally thought to cure hiccups? Try saying a tongue twister the next time you get hiccups.

Introduce a tongue twister by saying it very slowly and clearly, exaggerating the use of the articulators. Once the children can wrap their articulators around the words, increase the pace to see how rapidly the twister can be said without *tripping up*. The children will be able to increase the pace as they gain confidence. They will also be amused when a tangled tongue results in a mixed-up phrase!

Tongue Twisters to Twist the Tongue

Everyday Twisters

- Six selfish shellfish
- A big blue bucket of blue blueberries
- Double bubble gum bubbles double
- Two tooth sleuths
- Children chuckle cheerfully
- Blood red bed bugs
- Lazy lion lives alone
- Flee from the frog who flew from the fog
- "Snip with scissors," said the sister
- Bobby burst a bright balloon
- Ruth's tooth is loose
- A yellow yo-yo
- King Kong plays ping pong
- Three tree twigs
- Inchworm itching
- Gummy glue grew glum
- Fried fresh fish, fish fried fresh
- The queer quick quiz
- The shop sign shines
- Greek grapes
- A slapstick skit
- Kookie cool cookies
- Hiccup teacup

Seasonal Twisters

- The New Year is near
- A wild winter wind
- Velvet Valentines
- Toys for boys
- A selfish elf
- Santa's sleigh slipped on ice
- Excellent Easter eggs
- Funny bunnies
- Spring sings
- The wicked witch wished a wish
- Gruesome ghosts and goblins
- Pretty pumpkins
- Leaping latkes
- Nine nutcrackers gnawing at nuts
- Carolers carol clearly
- The reindeer ran around the rocks
- February flurries fleck the fences
- Fall's fabulous falling foliage

How many tongue twisters can you create?

Twisting with Tongue Twisters

Select a tongue twister that everyone knows, or familiarize the children with several of the tongue twisters included in this section before proceeding.

Repeat short twisters from three to ten times each. Repeat longer twisters two to three times each.

Assign each word of the twister to either one child or a small group of children. Recite the twister with each part spoken by a different child or group of speakers. Continue to repeat, picking up the pace with each repetition until a unified voice is created.

Pick up the pace once the children demonstrate confidence. For this to be successful, children will need to listen carefully to each other to pick up their cues, and to anticipate their turn.

Division One — Twisted Classmates

Have the children create tongue twisters using their names. For example:

Funny Floyd flipped flat flapjacks.

Practice saying the tongue twisters, adding appropriate expressive qualities to enhance the delivery. The children will likely come up with suggestions, such as slowing the tempo for some words, speeding up for others, raising and lowering pitch, and using variations in volume. The important thing is to give them opportunities to practice several versions until they are satisfied with the results.

Page 121

Children may also enjoy creating their own mini-book of selected tongue twisters, with illustrations for each. For examples of mini-books, refer to **Early Literacy — A Seasonal Approach**.

Division Two — Tangled Tales

Create a tongue twister story and illustrate it. Suggest that the children retell a familiar story as a tongue twister. For example:

- ***Three Peculiar Portly Pigs***
- ***Rude Red Riding Hood and the Really Ravenous Wolf***

Page 121

To introduce tongue twister stories, read **Princess Prunella and the Purple Peanut**, by Margaret Atwood. Or read other challenging stories that require careful attention to articulation, such as ***Rindercella and the Sass Glipper***, found in **Invitation to Readers Theatre:** *Celebrating Stories of our Canadian Heritage.*

After the children have completed their stories, practice reading the stories aloud without tripping over the alliteration.

Division Two — Twisted Commercials

Create a tongue twister commercial. One of my own students created this tricky commercial:

> Try Tony's tempting treats.
> The terrific taste will tantalize your taste buds.
> To order, send two toonies to:
> 222 Tatooine Street,
> Toronto, Ontario,
> T2T 2T2
>
> — Daniel Masliyah

Practice reading the commercials in a variety of voices appropriate to radio or television ads.

Playing with Poetry

Before reading the poem ***Pass the Peanut Butter***, do the following activities.

Page 63

Talk about Peanut Butter!

Ask the children to talk about their favorite foods, leading them into a discussion about peanut butter.

Encourage them to talk about peanut butter sandwiches. Ask how peanut butter feels in the mouth. Some children will no doubt express allergies to peanuts; however, there are other sandwiches that are relevant to this activity. Jam and honey have similar sticky properties, and it is the stickiness and *gooey-ness* that you want the children to understand and begin imitating.

Did you know that there are many claims about the origin of peanut butter?

Africans ground peanuts into stew as early as the 15th Century.

The Chinese have crushed peanuts into creamy sauces for centuries.

Civil War soldiers dined on peanut porridge.

Feel Sticky Peanut Butter!

Further explore the feeling of *stickiness* by involving the body. Imagine that the body is covered with peanut butter.

- Make different parts of the body stick together (hands together, hand to stomach, elbow to knee), and then work on pulling them apart.
- Pretend to attach one body part to the floor or the wall, and then pull away.

This exercise also assists relaxation, because children use tension to disengage themselves, and are more relaxed after the release.

Taste Peanut Butter!

To warm up the articulators, lead the children through a short imaginative exercise. Ask the children to mime the actions as you describe making a peanut butter sandwich.

Did you know that, in 1890, a food products company owner, George A. Bayle Jr., processed and packaged ground peanut paste as a nutritious substitute for people with poor teeth who could not chew meat?

- Open a loaf of bread and take out two slices, one at a time.
- Take a jar of peanut butter out of the cupboard, and open the lid. It may or may not be difficult to open.
- Reach into a drawer and take out a knife.
- Get a big gob of peanut butter from the jar, and spread it on the bread. Put the slices together and prepare to bite into it.
- Once they bite into the sandwich, a problem occurs. The peanut butter is *sooooo* sticky that they can't get the mouth open!
- Try screaming. What happens to the voice?
- Try to move the mouth around so it can open.

Encourage the children to really manipulate the face as they try to release the lips. Each child must find a way to open the mouth and solve the problem. Will the tongue be involved? Will they need to swallow several times? Will an imaginary glass of water help?

Read about Peanut Butter!

Page 63

Read the poem ***Pass the Peanut Butter***, by Marilyn Smith.

- How much does the speaker like peanut butter?
- Do you like any other food this much?
- Would you eat it anytime?

Provide the children with a script of the poem and read it together expressively.

Discussion and repeated reading personalizes understanding and adds to interpretation and presentation.

Read it again, experimenting with various approaches. How would the poem sound if the reader was:

- *Disgusted* by the thought of peanut butter?
- *Bored* with peanut butter?
- *Wild* about peanut butter?
- *Indifferent* to peanut butter?

The children will notice a difference in energy behind each reading, directly related to the attitude of the reader. This energy will affect the interpretation and delivery of the poem.

Pass the Peanut Butter

by Marilyn Smith

Reader 1	Peanu**t** bu**tt**er sandwiches
	are absolu**t**ely grea**t**!
Reader 2	Pu**t** them in my lunch bag
	or serve them on a pla**t**e.
Reader 3	Slice one up for breakfas**t**
	or dice one up for tea.
Reader 4	Peanu**t** bu**tt**er ANY**T**IME
	is fine with me.
Reader 1	One o'clock,
Reader 4	Two o'clock,
Reader 3	Three o'clock,
	or four —
ALL	PB is something I simply adore!
Reader 1	So — skip the chicken salad.
Reader 4	Don'**t** cu**t** up the cheese.
Reader 2	Jus**t** pass the peanu**t** bu**tt**er —
ALL	Pre**tt**y, pre**tt**y please!

Reprinted from ***Invitation to Readers Theatre:*** *A Guidebook for using Readers Theatre to celebrate holidays and special events throughout the year*, U-Otter-Read-It © 1997

Pronounce Peanut Butter!

Putting scripts on an overhead or in a pocket chart makes it convenient to quickly highlight specific sounds and words, in order to focus on articulation.

Put the following lines in a pocket chart (see below), or on an overhead projector:

> Peanu**t** bu**tt**er sandwiches are absolu**t**ely grea**t**!
> Pu**t** them in my lunch bag or serve them on a pla**t**e.

Example of a pocket chart with words of the poem on cards:

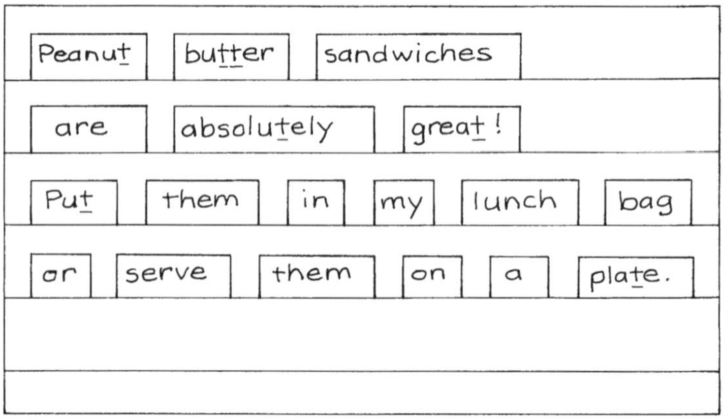

The script on page 63 has been printed with all plosive **t**s highlighted in bold type and underlined. This assists readers as they work on delivering the poem with clarity.

Why are all the **t** sounds underlined? Guide the children to understand that these are the sounds that tend to get missed, so underlining is used to highlight sounds that are especially important for clarity.

Show the following two lines, drawing attention to the letters that have been underlined.

> Just **p**ass the **p**eanut **b**utter —
> **P**retty, **p**retty **p**lease!

In this example, the plosive sounds are underlined to highlight the sounds that are often spoken with too little energy in the lips. This can ultimately lead to misunderstanding on the part of the listener, or and be interpreted as sloppy.

Caution: *Overdoing* articulation sounds fake and unnatural.

Experiment with different amounts of energy applied to the articulators to help the children recognize the effect on overall articulation. *Overdoing* articulation takes away from the success and enjoyment of a performance, because listeners are drawn to the sounds, rather than to the meaning of the text. The important goal is to develop an awareness of the need to be clear in order to be an effective communicator.

Perform Peanut Butter!

Repeat this tongue twister three times to warm up the articulators prior to performance:

Peanut butter is better by the pound.

Encourage the children to energize the lips on the **p** and **b** sounds.

Read the script together several times before assigning parts. Remind the children that they now have several techniques they can use to enhance the delivery of the poem.

To make the performance visually interesting, have each child cut a large piece of paper into the shape of a slice of bread. Paste a copy of the poem onto this paper slice of bread. The script can now be used as a prop. Having the script available gives children added confidence, since they do not have to rely on memory.

Using scripts as props adds to the visual effect of a performance.

Present the poem as follows:

- Repeat the warm-up activity, preparing the sandwich and biting into it.
- Recite the script. Add the chewing difficulties, as well as the excitement that would be expected from someone who *loves* peanut butter.
- At the end of the poem, the children can pretend to bite into their sandwiches again, further emphasizing their love for peanut butter!

See page 62

When speech sounds are clear and intelligible, the voice can be pulled from the back of the mouth, and placed out into the audience through **tone placement** and **tone projection**.

Tone Placement and Tone Projection

A man who expressed interest in my work told me about a telephone conversation with his elderly mother, who had been a teacher. After their greetings to each other, he told her that her voice sounded great (so powerful) — to which she firmly replied, "*How else would it sound? I practiced projecting it for over thirty years in the classroom!*"

Tone placement and **tone projection** are voice production techniques used in effective communication to make the speaker's voice reach the listener's ear in the best possible way.

STEP 7

Tone placement brings the sound to the front of the mouth, so that it can be projected a desired distance.

Often, sound is *caught* in the back of the mouth, making it difficult for others to hear. Physically, the tongue often humps up in the throat, producing a muffled sound. To correct this, it is helpful to *think* the sound forward, and to focus on the use of the front part of the mouth, especially the lips. In essence, the sound is *pulled* forward. This is called **tone placement**.

STEP 8

Once the sound reaches the front of the mouth, it can then be projected farther. This is called **tone projection**.

Placing the Tone Forward

By *thinking* the voice forward, the tone becomes clearer and resonance improves, because the sound fills the entire cavity of the mouth.

It is helpful to use a *visual cue* to direct the sound out of the back of the mouth. Children, especially, have difficulty understanding the *feeling* of tone placement. The following exercise for tone placement has been designed to help them *think* about sending the sound to the front of the mouth.

Learning with Lollipops

For this exercise, a Lifesaver™ lollipop works well, because of the hole in the middle of the candy. If a lollipop is not available, try a doughnut, tire, embroidery hoop, or hula hoop. Be creative! If no object is available, simply create a circle with your fingers.

Have the children stand facing the teacher. Remember good alignment! The teacher stands in front of the children, and holds up the lollipop.

Encourage the children to make an **ooooo** sound (as in *boot*), with the lips firmly rounded. Remembering good breath control, have them imagine directing the sound *through* the hole in the lollipop to the other side.

Focusing on a physical object helps children *aim* their voices to a particular point in the room.

It is important to avoid stretching the chin forward while doing this exercise, since that puts the body out of alignment. This causes tension in the both the throat and the vocal folds, which causes the pitch to rise. If this occurs, stop the exercise, and start again, emphasizing the need to keep the head relaxed and balanced at the top of the spine.

Repeat the exercise, using the following vowel sounds while keeping the voice comfortable and full:

- **ahhh** (as in *bat*)
- **eeee** (as in *beet*)
- **aiiii** (as in *bite*)
- **ohhh** (as in *boat*)

Once the vowel sounds have been mastered, expand the exercise by using such phrases as:

The cat sat on a mat.

Practicing Tone Projection

Once sound is placed properly, it is easier to project the voice to the back of the room.

The function of a projector is to enlarge a small image and to place that image onto a distant screen so that everyone can see it easily. In the same way, voices can be projected to a place at the back of a room. Since most children are familiar with projectors used in the classroom or in movie theatres, they may want to use that image as a reminder about how to project the voice.

Use a visual cue to help children further understand projection.

When children hold scripts, they have a tendency to direct the voice toward the paper, rather than toward the audience. The front row may be able to hear, but the voice may not reach the listeners at the back of the room. Remind the children to remember the audience at the back, and that everyone wants to hear the speaker. Give the children the opportunity to stand at the back of the room and listen while others speak. This encourages them to listen critically, and to become more aware of ways they can improve.

When working with children, it is a good idea for the teacher to stand at the back of the room. The physical distance between the teacher and the children directly influences the energy they use to project the voice. Having the teacher stand at the back of the room provides a visual cue to encourage the children to project.

Caution
Never push from the throat for projection. Use the stomach muscles (abdominal press) to support the energy needed to catapult the voice to the listener.

Abdominal press, page 39

Physically, projection NEVER comes from the throat. The power of the voice is driven by the muscles of exhalation, also referred to as the *abdominal press*. The abdominal muscles contract during exhalation, pushing against the diaphragm, which in turn drives the air out of the lungs. It is not necessary to place tension in the throat to produce sound. Screaming usually results from constricting the muscles of the throat, which places tension on the vocal folds, and causes a sore throat or voice loss. **Always remember that pain is an indicator of undesirable strain!**

Feeling the Power of the Voice

Have the children place their hands on their own stomach, and then quickly push in while releasing the sound **ohhh** (as in *boat*). They will notice a burst of sound as they do this. This is the area that adds power to the sound.

Use a visual cue as a quick reminder for breath correction.

Whenever it appears that breath support is lacking, the teacher can simply place a hand on his or her own stomach area. This visual cue reminds the children to use proper breath support, and to make the necessary physical adjustment to support the voice.

Use breathing exercises to strengthen the muscles of the abdomen. For example, the following exercises reinforce proper breathing, and strengthen projection:

- *Doggie Breath*, page 36
- *Bouncing Objects*, page 36

Projecting Snowballs

Linking a physical action to the concept of projection helps the children understand the idea of *throwing* the voice. Explore ways in which body actions either support or inhibit tone projection.

Have the children mime a snowball fight. Make the snowball, decide where the snowball will land, then prepare to throw it.

- Is it going across the room? To someone in particular?
- Depending on how far the snowball must go, will it need to be thrown really hard, or with only a little effort?

If a snowball is thrown with little or no energy, it will not travel very far. *Demonstrate this for the children.* To throw an object far requires greater energy in the body and the arm. *Demonstrate this for the children.* Throw the imaginary snowball with as much energy as possible, making observations about where the tension is strongest. Encourage the children to use the same kind of energy as they mime the snowball.

Re-creating that feeling of energy and placement of tension, add sounds to the action:

- **H ohhh** (as in *boat*)
- **H oooo** (as in *boot*)
- **H eeee** (as in *beet*)
- **H ayyy** (as in *bait*)
- **H aiii** (as in *bite*)

Adding an ***h*** before the vowel sound ensures connection to the breath.

With each throw, make the vowel sound travel through the air along with the snowball. After several repetitions, the children will begin to see this connection:

- The *stronger* the physical action, the *louder* the sound.
- The *weaker* the physical action, the *softer* the sound.

A word of caution: this activity can result in a shouting match. Remind the children **not** to scream as they project their vocal snowballs. If necessary, repeat the following activity to reinforce the use of the abdominal muscles.

Caution
Add power to the voice without screaming.

- *Feeling the Power of the Voice*, page 68

The Snowball

by Shirley Konrad

Use your hands as a shovel

And gather some snow.

Round it,

    Shape it,

        Pound it,

            Raise it,

Find your target and . . . THROW!

Playing with Poetry

This is an excellent activity to use as a warm-up prior to a performance in a large space, such as a school gymnasium.

Page 70

Introduce the poem ***The Snowball***. Read the poem a few times, asking the children to follow the directions by miming the actions. They will likely learn the words after a few repetitions.

At the end of the poem, on the word *THROW*, encourage them to project the voice as they mime throwing the snowball. Do this several times, until the children are warmed up.

A properly projected voice will feel comfortable, not forced. If, at any time, the voices need to be louder, use a visual cue, such a cupped hand behind the ear, to indicate "*louder.*" To remind them to support the voice properly, place a hand on the stomach. The children will remember that the power to project comes from the center of the body.

Visual cues quickly remind children to *project* the voice.

Tone placement and tone projection are the last steps in producing the voice effectively, and can be done properly only if all the voice production steps have been addressed, and the children have understood and internalized them.

Putting It All Together

A single piece of literature can be used to combine all aspects of voice production into one exercise. This exercise is an excellent way to review and reinforce all the steps in voice production, and their relationship to each other.

Teachers are encouraged to examine literature from a vocal perspective, and to be creative in designing lessons for their students. Each poem will provide different opportunities for exploring the steps in voice production.

Lazy Jane, by Shel Silverstein, on page 74, is an example of a simple poem that can be used to achieve these objectives. The focus of this poem is the word *lazy*, so this word becomes the starting point for the exercise.

Playing with Poetry

Lazy Thoughts

Discussing concepts prior to saying the poem explores common experiences.

Write the word *lazy* on the board or on a flash card. Ask the children to say the word, and to give ideas about the meaning of the word. Guide them with questions such as:

- When do you feel the laziest? On the weekend? After school? During the summer?
- What does lazy *feel* like? Does the body goes limp? Do you feel like doing anything? Do you want to sleep?
- What do you tend to do when you are feeling lazy? Nothing? Watch television? Sleep on the couch?

Relaxation

Lazy Feelings

Checklist for Proper Floor Placement, page 24

Have the children lie comfortably, in their own space, on the floor. Check to ensure that children are in the proper position.

Think about being lazy.

- How does lazy *look*?
- How does lazy *feel*?

As the children think about laziness, they will relax the body.

Relaxation, page 19

To increase the feeling of relaxation, guide them to stretch the body from wall to wall in the following way:

- Reach toward one wall with the hands and arms, and stretch the legs and feet toward the opposite wall. This tightens the muscles throughout the body.
- Hold this stretched position for three (3) seconds to register the feeling.
- Now go totally limp.

Ask the children to describe how these two positions feel. Expect words such as *tight*, *tense*, *rigid*, and *stiff* when describing the stretch, and *loose*, *floppy*, *light*, *limp*, and *listless* when describing what happens when they go limp.

Do the stretching sequence again. This time, when relaxing, take time to *melt* into the floor. Breathe deeply, then exhale with an audible sigh. Encourage the children to sigh with an open and free **awww** sound (as in *ball*).

Concentrate on the stomach, and center the breath into this area. This allows the body to open up along the floor, and loosens the back muscles. Breathing deeply further relaxes the body.

Lazy Problem

While the children are relaxed, present the following scenario.

When you are lazy, you don't feel like doing anything. If you were very, very thirsty, but were too lazy to get yourself a glass of water, how would you solve the problem?

- Would you call your mother to bring you a glass of water?
- Suppose no one is at home. What else might work?
- The dog's dish is full of water! Would you take it from there?

Lazy Solution

After the children have given their suggestions, read aloud the poem ***Lazy Jane***, by Shel Silverstein, on page 74, and ask them to listen for Jane's creative solution to this dilemma.

Read the poem aloud several times, inviting the children to join in as they learn the words. Ask them to notice how many times the words *lazy* and *wait* are said (6 *lazys* and 5 *waits*).

LAZY JANE

Lazy
lazy
lazy
lazy
lazy
lazy
Jane,
she
wants
a
drink
of
water
so
she
waits
and
waits
and
waits
and
waits
and
waits
for
it
to
rain.

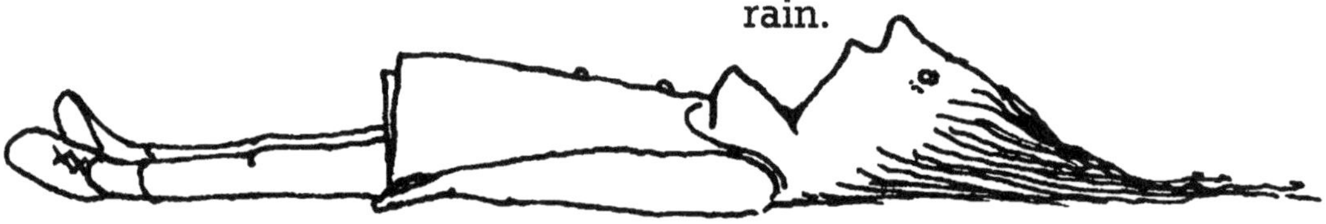

Breathing, page 34

Identify the breathing spots in the poem ***Lazy Jane***:

- Opening breath to begin the poem
- One breath after *Jane*
- Another breath after *so*
- Final breath at the end after *rain*

Show the poem on an overhead, with the breath spots clearly inserted. The symbol ♭ indicates that a breath should be taken. Ask the children to breathe *only* in these spots as they say the poem together.

By coordinating breathing, the delivery becomes smoother and more fluent. Each breath needs to be deep enough to cover a long phrase. It is also desirable to practice *breathing in* without gasping audibly. Audible inhalation is an indication of tension in the upper chest area.

Phonation, page 43

To relax the throat muscles, suggest that Jane might be *soooo* tired that she feels the urge to yawn a couple of times. Say the poem together, inviting the children to yawn along with Jane! Don't stifle the yawn — let the yawn release freely. The body relaxes further, so the sound initiated after the yawn will be free and open. Encourage the children to notice what happens to the body after yawning. Listen to the difference in voice quality, and notice the difference in energy level.

Resonance, page 47

Guide the children with the following suggestions, leading them towards a sensory (feel, taste) awareness of rain:

> Here it comes — feel it slip down your throat. Enjoy the taste. How refreshing! You are so happy to quench your thirst . . . and with such little effort!

Encourage the children to let out a long and pleasurable **mmmmm** sound. Feel the sound as it vibrates throughout the whole body.

Articulation, page 51

To increase the flexibility of the tongue tip for clear articulation of the **l** sound in the word *lazy*, repeat the following, stressing the **l**s:

- la, la, la, la, la, la, la
- lee, lee, lee, lee, lee, lee, lee
- la, lee, la, lee, la, lee, la

Repeat the exercise, substituting **t**s for the **l**s.

Say the poem again, making sure the **t** in the word *water* is clearly articulated. When the children reach the end of the poem, ask them to drop the jaw loosely, like Jane has, as if waiting for the rain to fall into the mouth.

Tone Placement and Tone Projection, page 66

Have the children lie on the floor in a comfortable position. Ask them to open their eyes, and imagine rain clouds above them. Repeat the poem, directing the voice toward the rain clouds.

Encourage the children to connect to the word *lazy*, and make each repetition of the word slightly different, yet meaningful. Consider exploring variations in pitch and inflection, extending vowel sounds, and colouring words.

Alignment, page 25

When the previous exercise is completed, have the children move to a comfortable standing position. Rather than jumping up off the floor, ask the children to roll up from the floor into proper alignment by slowly rolling through the spine and the neck, with the head coming up last. This needs to be done slowly, with the children focusing on lengthening and opening the body. Once in a standing position, they will feel tall, refreshed, and energized.

When all aspects of voice production have been understood, practiced, and internalized, children will be ready to further explore the elements that create dynamic and expressive voices.

Vocal Expression

When children are able to produce and maintain strong, clear, rich and well-supported voices, they will then be able to explore vocal expression. The vocal expression techniques in this section can be addressed **in any sequence**. These techniques include:

- Pause and Phrasing
- Pace
- Pitch
- Inflection
- Emphasis
- Colouring
- Volume

Symbols

Visual cues are important for representing abstract ideas. Written symbols that represent expression techniques can be used easily with children while they work with their scripts. Symbols to guide the reader have been inserted throughout this section.

Introducing visual cues early enhances the use and understanding of vocal techniques.

Very short pause

Short pause

Long pause

Continue to the next line using a suspensary pause

Increase pace

Decrease pace

Draw out the vowels

Higher pitch

Lower pitch

Rising inflection

Falling inflection

Underline for emphasis

Colouring

Louder

Softer

Pause and Phrasing

Symbols for **pause**:

- ⁄ Very short pause
- / Short pause
- // Long pause
- ◡ Continue to the next line using a suspensary pause

Pause is one of the most important techniques for vocal expression. A pause is a noticeable break, rather than just a hesitation.

Pauses provide many benefits. A pause:

- Helps the reader replenish the breath supply
- Gives the reader time to think about the content
- Allows the reader to make sense of the script so that the listener can follow and understand
- Provides an opportunity for the listener to reflect, internalize, and personalize the words
- Creates emphasis for important text

Phrasing is the grouping of words to form a thought or idea. Phrasing occurs more easily when readers trust their interpretation of meaning, and are confident about how the words fit together.

Using pauses contributes to successful phrasing. In printed texts, punctuation marks visually indicate the separation of phrases, and a reader may pause to acknowledge these marks. A good reader understands the relationship between pauses and phrasing, and uses these techniques to communicate the text effectively.

Cause to Pause

Children often pause at the end of a line of poetry, whether or not there is a punctuation mark. This practice results in an undesirable *sing-song* or choppy effect.

Read the following stanza from ***The Tale of the Worms***, by Gwen Molnar, adding a short pause (/) where indicated.

Page 88

The rains came down /
The worms came out /
The worms came out /
To play /
They were skinny and pink /
And made everyone think /
They'd forgotten to dress /
That day.

By stopping at the end of every line, the rhythm of the poem becomes exaggerated, and tends to overpower the meaning. This rhythmic feel of poetry can overshadow the need to think about and connect to the meaning of the words. This unpleasant reading style is likely one reason that so many people grow up to dislike poetry. However, by varying both *length* and *types* of pauses, the reader creates phrasing that focuses on the meaning.

Reading poetry well requires effective use of pauses to indicate phrasing.

Length of Pauses

Generally, there are three possible lengths for a pause:

- Very short pause /
- Short pause /
- Long pause //

Encourage readers to explore the effect created by pauses of different lengths.

A **very short pause** (/) is so short that it is barely noticeable. This pause is a slight hold in which *no breath is taken.*

A **short pause** (/) is slightly longer than a very short pause, and is therefore more noticeable. One *may or may not take a breath,* depending on the need for one.

A **long pause** (//) is very noticeable because *a breath is always taken.* A long pause indicates a transition into a new thought or idea. New ideas or thoughts require a fresh breath, since the breath helps the reader energize and add meaning to the new phrase.

It is easy to get carried away with the timing of the pauses. Good readers have an intuitive sense about the length of pause needed to deepen the meaning.

NOTE
Be careful not to get carried away with the timing of pauses. Allow them to occur as naturally as possible.

Types of Pauses

Three types of pauses are used in poetry:

- Printer's pause or punctuation pause
- Caesura pause
- Suspensary pause

Printer's Pause or Punctuation Pause

Printer's pauses assist with conveying the meaning intended by the author.

Printer's pauses or **punctuation pauses** are the printed symbols that writers use to assist readers with meaning. When a punctuation mark follows a word, the reader places a pause after the word. However, punctuation pauses do not have to be of equal length.

End punctuation indicates the completion of a thought. The length can vary between a short pause and a long pause, and a breath is usually taken. End punctuation includes:

- Period
- Question mark
- Exclamation mark

Punctuation within a sentence indicates a separation of words and phrases to clarify meaning. The words within a phrase fit together as a unit, but the phrase itself may require a slight separation from the rest of the sentence. Since the phrases are connected to the sentence as a whole, a very short pause or a short pause is appropriate. Too long a pause contributes to a disjointed reading. Punctuation within a sentence includes:

- Comma
- Semicolon
- Colon
- Dash
- Ellipsis (. . .)
- Parentheses
- Quotation marks

Page 83

The excerpts on the next page, taken from the poem ***Puddle Muddle***, by Marilyn Smith, illustrate examples of punctuation pauses. Notice the variations of length and position of the pauses.

There's mud on my hands and mud up my nose. /

Period .

A period indicates a pause that is longer in duration than a comma. A short pause here places emphasis on the word *nose*.

Maybe she'll laugh and remember way back
to her raincoat, / umbrella / and rubbers.

Comma ,

A short pause separates the items in the list and gives each word focus. The reader can then add greater vocal variety to the delivery.

It crept up behind — / there was no time to flee!

Dash —

A short pause separates the thoughts and feelings, adding emotion.

Will she know about spring / (and the danger it brings), /
with puddles that like to give cuddles?

Parentheses ( )

A short pause is needed before and after text in parentheses, coupled with an increase in pace, makes the subordinate phrase in parentheses less important than the dominant phrase.

Do you think she'll believe in puddles that fly? //

Question Mark ?

The audience can seriously consider the question only if given enough time to think about it. A long pause provides that time.

People are starting to stop and stare! //

Exclamation Mark !

A long pause heightens the emotion of the statement.

Caesura Pause

A **caesura pause** (pronounced *say-zhoor-uh*) occurs within a line of poetry. This kind of pause is found through the rhythm of the line, is unmarked, and is often described as a *felt* pause. A caesura pause is a slight hold or a *very* short pause (⁄), and no breath is taken. If a breath is taken, the phrasing becomes choppy.

It's even oozing ⁄ between my toes!

The slight hold is taken after the word *oozing*. This pause emphasizes and adds meaning to the word, capturing the slowness of *oozing*.

In great gobs of grime ⁄ that drop from the sky?

This slight pause after the phrase *great gobs of grime* emphasizes the descriptive words, and allows the listener to form a vivid image.

Suspensary Pause

A **suspensary pause** is a slight pause taken at the end of a line of poetry where there is no punctuation mark, and the idea continues to the next line. The voice is suspended ON the word, rather than AFTER it, to maintain the integrity of meaning. A suspensary pause is NOT about creating suspense; instead, it momentarily suspends the line ending in order to acknowledge the structure of the poem. No fresh breath is taken on a suspensary pause.

Use this symbol (⌣) to indicate a suspensary pause as you continue to the next line.

> Now I'm covered in goo and there's nothing to do ⌣
> but go in and talk to my mother.

Suspending the word *do* connects the action to the impending reaction.

> Maybe she'll laugh and remember way back ⌣
> to her raincoat, umbrella and rubbers.

Suspend the word *back* and continue without taking a breath. The suspensary pause not only acknowledges the structure of the poem, but also connects the list of items to the mother's childhood memories.

Visual Pauses

Use of visual cues reminds children to pause.

Introduce children to the use of visual cues to indicate placement and length of pauses. For example, a raised hand can signify a stop, or can control the timing of a pause.

There is a natural tendency for children to rush the pace when reading in front of an audience. To better control that tendency, introduce readers to all three types of pauses, and encourage them to mark their scripts accordingly. This will remind the readers to take the time to pause, in order to produce a more meaningful — and therefore more effective — performance. The children will begin to mark their own scripts as they come to recognize the value of delivering carefully prepared oral presentations.

> Remember that pauses are used to develop phrasing, which affects interpretation of the text. Remind children that pauses are important for the speaker as well as the listener.

Puddle Muddle

by Marilyn Smith

Reader 1	There's mud on my hands and mud up my nose.
Reader 2	It's even oozing between my toes!
Reader 3	It's dripping and dropping from strands of hair.
Reader 4	People are starting to stop and stare!
Reader 2	But the mud puddle flew all over me.
Reader 3	It crept up behind — there was no time to flee!
Reader 4	Now I'm covered in goo and there's nothing to do but go in and talk to my mother.
Reader 1	Do you think she'll believe in puddles that fly? In great gobs of grime that drop from the sky?
Reader 4	Will she know about spring (and the danger it brings), with puddles that like to give cuddles?
Reader 2	Maybe she'll laugh and remember way back to her raincoat, umbrella and rubbers,
Reader 3	and I'll jump in the tub,
Reader 1	and she'll help me scrub,
Reader 4	while we chat about sneaky, mud puddles!

Reprinted from ***Invitation to Readers Theatre:*** *A Guidebook for using Readers Theatre to celebrate holidays and special events throughout the year*, U-Otter-Read-It © 1997

Pace

Symbols for **pace**:

⟶ Increase pace

⟵ Decrease pace

Pace, or rate, is the speed at which we speak. Pace is generally classified as *fast*, *medium*, or *slow*. When *all* the lines are delivered using the same pace, the material becomes dull and lifeless. Varying the pace livens the material being presented, and makes it more interesting for the listener.

When expressing feelings, pace and pitch often work closely together. For example, excitement or anxiety is often conveyed by using a faster pace and a higher pitch. In contrast, sadness or reverence is often conveyed by using a slower pace and a lower pitch.

How Is Pace Determined?

Pace helps to convey meaning, mood, and climax.

It is important to explore the subtleties and complexities of a selection of text to determine the pace changes that best convey the meaning. The following questions, with very general suggestions, will assist in determining the appropriate pace for a piece.

- How does ***mood*** determine pace?

  In general, slow down the pace if the selection is sad or reflective. If it is happy or exciting, increase the pace.

- Does the piece build to a ***climax***?

  If so, pick up the pace to convey excitement and anticipation, or slow down the pace to convey suspense.

- What is the best pace for conveying the ***meaning*** of the line or phrase?

  Use a slower pace for the important lines and phrases that contribute significantly to overall meaning. Use a faster pace for subordinate phrases, which are less important.

Children have a natural tendency to speak quickly. Reading aloud will help to slow down the pace due to the nature of the task. It is important to emphasize to the children the effect that pace has on the listener's understanding of, and response to, the material.

Pace affects the listener's understanding and response.

- A pace that is *too slow* affects the listener's focus, and may cause restlessness and impatience.
- A pace that is *too fast* affects the listener's ability to catch details. Clarity suffers because words are rushed, and sounds are missed.

Slowing Down the Pace

There are two effective ways to slow down, or decrease, the pace.

1. **Add more pauses.**

   Children are often afraid to lose momentum in their reading, so they run lines together, and forget to use pauses. The use of written pause symbols (/́ , / , //) on scripts reminds the children to pause, and assists with pace. Reinforce the dramatic power of pausing, because pauses contribute to strengthening understanding, meaning, and overall impact.

Pause and Phrasing, page 78

Two ways to slow down the pace:
- Add more pauses.
- Elongate the sounds.

2. **Elongate the sounds.**

   Another tendency is for children to speak with short, clipped sounds. By drawing out the vowel sounds (⟷), it is easier to give full value to these sounds, and to slow down the overall pace. This is a particularly effective technique to use when dealing with material that has the potential to surprise or shock the listener.

Picking Up the Pace

There are two effective ways to pick up, or increase, the pace.

1. **Focus on clarity.**

   Too fast a pace negatively affects the clarity of sounds and words. Remember to maintain clarity of speech when increasing pace. A rapid pace must not overshadow meaning. Articulation exercises are valuable tools for helping to establish a balance between pace and clarity.

Articulation, page 51

Two ways to increase the pace:
- Focus on clarity.
- Add vocal energy.

2. **Add vocal energy.**

   Controlled energy behind the words gives the *illusion* of picking up the pacc without sacrificing clarity. To do this, use proper breath support, and intensify the involvement of both voice and body.

Breathing, page 34

Playing with Poetry

Page 88

Expressively read ***The Tale of the Worms***, by Gwen Molnar. The way in which the poem is initially read aloud serves as a model for the children to follow.

Use the following suggestions to apply changes of pace to the poem. These excerpts are marked with pace symbols only, since that is the focus. However, consider using other expressive techniques to strengthen the elements of the story, and mark the script to reflect those elements.

Repeated practice reinforces and strengthens literacy skills.

Analyzing different aspects of the script gives readers many opportunities to revisit the text, thereby strengthening literacy skills, as well as further strengthening comprehension of the story-line and the characters.

Poem Excerpts	Suggestions for Pace
← The rains came down	**Mood** Imagine a rainy, dreary day. Read the first line slowly to capture that mood. Elongate the vowels in the words to convey the essence of a dreary day.
The worms came out To play They were skinny and pink	**Character** Visualize the worms. A medium pace works well here. Colour the words *skinny* and *pink*.
→ They wriggled off In a long, thin line In a long, thin line They went.	**Action and Feeling** The worms are excited about the rain as they wriggle through the streets. Increase the pace to convey excitement, while colouring the word *l-o-n-g*.
← Inside the tent Four fishermen sat Four fishermen sat So blue, They had no more bait So they'd have to wait Till the worst of the rain Was through.	**Feeling** *Blue* in this context means *sad* or *melancholy*. To convey this feeling, slow the pace. Using a lower pitch will also suggest how frustrated the fishermen feel about waiting out the rain.

Symbols, page 77

Colouring, page 106

Pitch, page 90

→
The worms looked up
The men looked down
The men looked down
And cheered,
"Here's the bait we need!"
And with lightning speed
On their hooks the worms
Were speared.

Climax
Build pace through this part to create the feeling of anticipation and excitement. When the men see the worms, they seize their opportunity with zest! Increase vocal energy and pace to capture that feeling. Colour words such as *cheered* by raising the pitch, and *speared* by lowering the pitch and stressing the downward action.

→
The fish were caught
All ate the worms
All ate the worms
In two;

Action
Eating is an aggressive action. Show this by increasing the pace throughout this section.

Mood, character, action, feeling, climax, and setting are story elements that affect choices for pacing.

→
The worms then turned
And swiftly home
And swiftly home
They sped,

Action
Building on the previous action, increase the pace. Add vocal energy to convey a *swift* quality without speeding through the words.

←
And they climbed the stairs
And they said their prayers,
And crawled thankfully
Back to bed.

Setting
The worms are glad to be back to the peaceful, safe environment of their home. Slow the pace of the final lines to indicate this contentment. Elongate the vowels in words such as *thankfully* and *bed* to help the listener identify with the comforts of home, and to increase the impact of this delightful ending.

Pace is affected by the emotions, intentions, and meaning attached to the reading. Added vocal energy can be interpreted as an increase in pace. The ability to add vocal energy decreases the risk of sloppy articulation that often occurs when children rush to get through their part.

The Tale of the Worms

by Gwen Molnar

Reader 1	The rains came down
Reader 2	The worms came out
Readers 3 & 4	The worms came out
	To play
Reader 2	They were skinny and pink
Reader 1	And made everyone think
	They'd forgotten to dress
	That day.
Reader 4	They wriggled off
Reader 3	In a long, thin line
Readers 2 & 4	In a long, thin line
	They went.
Reader 1	Over sidewalks and drains
Reader 3	Over cobbles and lanes
Reader 4	Till they came to the door
	Of a tent.
Reader 2	Inside the tent
Reader 3	Four fishermen sat
Readers 2 & 4	Four fishermen sat
	So blue,
Reader 1	They had no more bait
Reader 4	So they'd have to wait
Reader 3	Till the worst of the rain
	Was through.

Reprinted from ***Invitation to Readers Theatre:*** *A Guidebook for using Readers Theatre to celebrate holidays and special events throughout the year,* U-Otter-Read-It © 1997

The Tale of the Worms, continued

Reader 1	The worms looked up
Reader 3	The men looked down
Reader 4	The men looked down
	And cheered,
Reader 2	"Here's the bait we need!"
Reader 1	And with lightning speed
Readers 2 & 3	On their hooks the worms
	Were speared.
Reader 4	The fish were caught
Reader 1	All ate the worms
Readers 2 & 3	All ate the worms
	In two;
Reader 4	But the other half
	Of the worms just laughed
Reader 2	For a whole new half
	They grew.
Reader 1	The worms then turned
Reader 2	And swiftly home
Readers 3 & 4	And swiftly home
	They sped,
Reader 2	And they climbed the stairs
Reader 4	And they said their prayers,
Reader 2	And crawled thankfully
	Back to bed.

Reprinted from ***Invitation to Readers Theatre:*** *A Guidebook for using Readers Theatre to celebrate holidays and special events throughout the year,* U-Otter-Read-It © 1997

Pitch

Symbols for **pitch**:

∧ Higher pitch

∨ Lower pitch

Pitch is the level at which we speak. Pitch levels are usually categorized as *high*, *medium*, or *low*.

A child's voice is often freer than an adult's voice, unless the adult has been encouraged to develop and maintain a flexible pitch range. Maturity, self-consciousness, and aging tend to reduce expressiveness in voices, thus limiting the speaking range.

The human voice is capable of achieving many pitch levels. Observe a child playing with a toy, such as a stuffed animal or a doll. Listen to the playful ways in which the child talks, experimenting with high, medium, and low pitches, depending on the particular attributes of the toy. It is this freedom that we want to encourage in reading aloud.

Vocal folds, page 43

Emphasize the need to relax the throat properly for the best voice production, since pitch is determined by the physical state of the vocal folds.

- Thin, short vocal folds that are too tense usually produce a higher, squeakier voice.
- Thick, long vocal folds that are too relaxed usually produce a lower, huskier voice.

Connecting Pitch to Emotions

We tend to associate pitch levels with emotions, and we respond accordingly.

- **Higher Pitch Range**
  Feelings such as joy, excitement, and humour tend to be associated with a higher pitch range. Anger and fear can also be conveyed by a high pitch.
- **Lower Pitch Range**
  Emotions such as sadness, melancholy, and worry tend to be associated with a lower pitch range. Moods that are dark, mysterious, haunting, or lonely are best conveyed with deeper tones.
- **Optimum Pitch**
  This is the level at which we speak, or our most comfortable pitch level. Optimum pitch can be used for narration between dialogue, and for information that is factual, or requires little or no emotional connection.

Consider the mood of each of the following poem excerpts, and identify the pitch most appropriate to express each one. To assist with choice of pitch, quickly scan the selection to see which words *pop out*, giving clues to the appropriate pitch range.

Poem Excerpts	**Suggestions for Pitch**	
∨ Outside, the wind is raging the snow is swirling round. Inside, my head is yearning to know you're safe and sound. Outside, the sun is setting and darkness starts to creep. Inside my mind I ponder, as worry prevents my sleep.	Speaking in the lower pitch range conveys the mood of the *raging wind* and *swirling snow*. Because these actions suggest chaos and confusion, a bright, cheery voice would probably not be suitable. Other words that suggest the use of a lower pitch include *darkness*, *creep*, and *worry*.	***The Storm***, **Early Literacy — A Seasonal Approach** **Bibliography**, page 121
∧ Love comes — in bright smiles, in twinkling eyes, in gentle hugs, in lullabies.	Speaking in a higher, lighter pitch suggests a happier, warmer mood. Words such as *love*, *bright*, *twinkling*, *gentle*, and *lullabies* reinforce the choice of this lighter pitch.	***Love Comes***, **Early Literacy — A Seasonal Approach** **Bibliography**, page 121

Exploring Pitch Range

Explore pitch range with the children. How many different pitch levels can they discover?

- Count from 1 to 8, starting at the lowest comfortable pitch, and moving to the highest comfortable pitch.

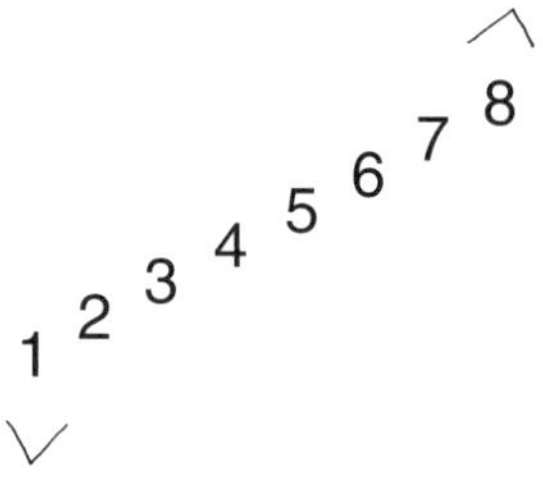

These pitches will not necessarily move evenly, as pitches in music. The goal is to have the children explore their range, and to go beyond the boundaries of their normal speaking range.

- Expand the counting from 1 to 12, and then from 1 to 16.
- Reverse the pattern, going backwards from 16 to 1 (highest to lowest pitch).

Caution
Avoid moving the head to indicate change of pitch.

Caution the children against their natural tendency to move the head and chin in relation to the direction of the pitch (up or down). Such movements stretch or compress the vocal folds unnecessarily.

If possible, do this exercise with a pitched musical instrument to provide the children with more guidance in finding their pitch range.

Character Voices

Vary the pitch to explore characterization.

Effective storytellers use a variety of pitches to give life to the *voices* of different characters. In familiar fairy tales, for example, characters will be recognized by the pitch and voice quality used by the storyteller. Consider the following:

- The Wolf in ***The Three Little Pigs*** will use a deep pitch, combined with a gruff quality.
- The small, medium, and large goats in ***The Three Billy Goats Gruff*** will use pitches related to their size and status.
- The Giant in ***Jack and the Beanstalk*** will use a deep pitch with a full, threatening volume.
- The Witch in ***Hansel and Gretel*** will use a high pitch, combined with a crackly quality.

Experiment with these voices, then have the children hold conversations with each other, using the voices of the characters.

The children will discover that pitch assists characterization. Further explore pitch by talking about voices that are associated with different characters and personalities. What kinds of characters use high voices? Low voices? Medium voices?

For example, excited, giddy, or tiny characters often speak in higher pitches, while gloomy, grumpy, and larger characters often speak in lower pitches. Consider which voices would be used for Piglet, Eeyore, and Winnie-the-Pooh.

Playing with Poetry

Examine the lines for each of the eight reindeer in ***Reindeer Chatter***, by Marilyn Smith.

An initial reading of this script will likely result in *weak* or *flat* characters. However, explore the possibilities for capturing the character and attitude of each reindeer, using the suggestions given below as a starting point. This type of exploration is especially helpful when there is only limited information given about a character. Readers will add their own interpretation to each character, producing a more interesting and entertaining delivery for the audience.

Exploring character strengthens comprehension and enhances interpretation.

Page 95

Inflection, page 96

	Poem Excerpts	**Suggestions for Pitch**
∨	Eight little reindeer in a great big hurry, stomped their hooves to cause quite a flurry.	Use inflections to vary the pitch throughout this stanza. *Stomped* and *flurry* suggest anxiety and impatience. A lower pitch gives greater meaning to the feeling and action.
	The first reindeer said,	Use an optimum pitch level (normal speaking voice) for all narration between dialogue.
∧	"It's nearly Christmas day!"	The exclamation mark indicates excitement — Reindeer 1 can hardly wait for Christmas! Finding a voice in the upper pitch range may convey this feeling.
∨	"Let's hook up the sleigh."	Reindeer 2 sees work to be done, and he's also giving orders to the others. A lower pitch might be suitable to convey his authority, and to command attention from the other reindeer.
∧	"The children will be sleeping!"	Reindeer 3 expresses concern about the children. A slightly higher, softer pitch may be an effective way to show a comforting and caring attitude.

Poem Excerpts	Suggestions for Pitch
"Onto rooftops, we'll be leaping."	Reindeer 4 might be a bit of a risk-taking superhero, so a voice in the lower pitch range would seem to be the most appropriate. On the other hand, this reindeer may be leaping for the first time — is he scared? Excited? Timid? How will each feeling affect the pitch?
"The presents are all ready."	Reindeer 5 makes a statement. Use a pitch that reflects how he feels about this accomplishment. Elated? Exhausted? Relieved?
"Our load is very heavy."	Reindeer 6 may feel anxious about the long journey ahead, or he may be cautioning the others of the need to work hard. The seriousness of either feeling calls for a lower pitch. How would the pitch change if this reindeer were bragging about the heavy load?
"To each home, we will fly!"	The exclamation mark indicates an intensity of feeling. Perhaps Reindeer 7 is proud to be one of Santa's reindeer. A strong, medium-high pitch, using vocal energy, might indicate pride.
"In the twinkling of an eye."	Reindeer 8 refers confidently to the magic of their awesome task. The word *twinkling* captures the magic, and may be best conveyed with a higher pitch.

Remember that pitch is created by the vibrations in the vocal folds. By avoiding tension in the neck and throat muscles, the pitch range will be more flexible and easier to control.

Reindeer Chatter

by Marilyn Smith

Chorus	Eight little reindeer in a great big hurry, stomped their hooves to cause quite a flurry.
Chorus	The first reindeer said,
Reader 1	"It's nearly Christmas day!"
Chorus	The second reindeer said,
Reader 2	"Let's hook up the sleigh."
Chorus	The third reindeer said,
Reader 3	"The children will be sleeping!"
Chorus	The fourth reindeer said,
Reader 4	"Onto rooftops, we'll be leaping."
Chorus	The fifth reindeer said,
Reader 5	"The presents are all ready."
Chorus	The sixth reindeer said,
Reader 6	"Our load is very heavy."
Chorus	The seventh reindeer said,
Reader 7	"To each home, we will fly!"
Chorus	The eighth reindeer said,
Reader 8	"In the twinkling of an eye."
Chorus	So in jumped Santa with a
Santa	"Ho, Ho, Ho!"
Chorus	Calling "Merry Christmas!" to the world down below.

Reprinted from ***Invitation to Readers Theatre:*** *A Guidebook for using Readers Theatre to celebrate holidays and special events throughout the year*, U-Otter-Read-It © 1997

Inflection

Inflection is the change of pitch on a single word or syllable. Since inflection adds emotional meaning to a word, it directly affects the listener's understanding of what is being said.

Types of Inflections

Symbols for **inflection**:

Rising inflection

Falling inflection

Generally, there are three types of inflections:

- Rising inflection
- Falling inflection
- Circumflex inflection

Each type of inflection communicates a variety of emotions and meanings.

Going Up

UPWARD

- curiosity
- doubt
- insecurity

The **rising** or **upward inflection** ( ) occurs when the voice glides or rises upward. This inflection can indicate a question, curiosity, or doubt. When used at the end of a line, a rising inflection suggests that the thought is incomplete. It may also suggest a thought that trails away, leaving an audience hanging in anticipation of more to follow.

Be cautious in overusing the rising inflection, especially if the intention is to complete an idea. Girls are likely to use more upward inflections than boys. This may be interpreted as a lack of security and confidence, thus weakening the effect of what the individual has to say. Confident speakers, on the other hand, often end statements with a downward inflection, and are more likely to command an attentive audience.

Going Down

DOWNWARD

- certainty
- finality
- command

The **downward** or **falling inflection** ( ) occurs when the voice glides or falls downward to a lower pitch. This inflection can indicate a complete thought, certainty, or a sense of finality, as in giving a command or making a forceful statement.

Going Up and Down (or Down and Up!)

A **circumflex** or **double inflection** combines the above two inflections. The voice glides up and then down, or down and then up, depending on the intended meaning. This inflection can indicate some form of sarcasm, mocking, or doubt.

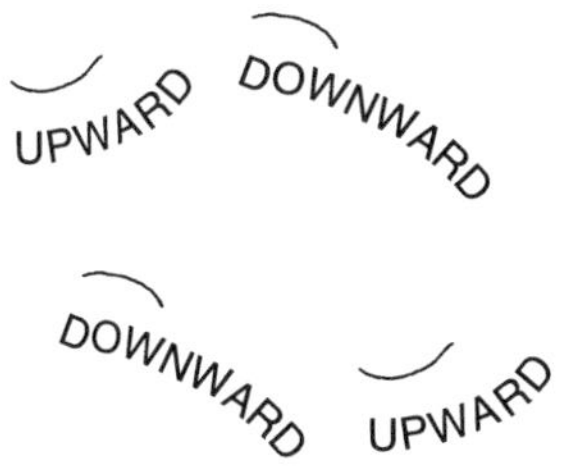

- sarcasm
- mocking
- doubt

Length of Inflections

Inflections can vary in length, depending on the emotional content.

When expressing positive feelings such as joy, surprise, and wonder, the inflection is usually longer in duration. This is accomplished by elongating the vowel sound(s) of the word.

The length of an inflection is affected by negative or positive emotions.

When expressing negative feelings such as anger, impatience, or intense frustration, the inflection is usually shorter in duration, with clipped and abrupt vowel sound(s).

Vocal Roller Coaster

To explore inflection, place children in a circle, and have each child in turn say **oh** in a different way. Set the scene by first suggesting an emotional context for the word **oh**. For example, suppose you have received a gift. How would you say **oh** if you were surprised by the gift? Disappointed? Excited? Indifferent?

For more possibilities to further explore the types of inflection, mix and match the words and emotions from the chart below.

Emotions, page 127

Word List	Emotion List
no well whatever hello because thanks hey mine	surprise anger disappointment joy fear curiosity mistrust clueless

Expand the exercise with phrases. For example:

I know that.

She said what?

Punctuation and Inflections

Punctuation marks indicate the appropriate inflection.

Reinforce the way punctuation marks guide the reader to use the appropriate inflection. For example:

- A **question mark** (**?**) means that the voice glides up to communicate curiosity, wonder, uncertainty, an incomplete thought, or doubt.
- A **period** (**.**) means that the voice glides downward to communicate a complete thought, certainty, or a simple demand.
- An **exclamation mark** (**!**) means that the voice definitely glides down to communicate the intensity of the meaning or feeling expressed, or a forceful demand.
- An **ellipsis** (**. . .**) can indicate an incomplete thought, or an extension of the feeling expressed. The voice rises up slightly to hold the meaning.
- A **dash** (**—**) usually holds the previous thought or feeling — then adds more to it. The voice rises slightly to indicate the continuation of the idea.

Number Talk

This activity helps the children understand that changes in inflection reveal the intention behind the words.

Use numbers, nonsense words, or sounds to focus on inflection rather than meaning.

Divide the children into pairs, with one child as **A** and the other as **B**. Ask them to create a conversation with each other, using numbers between 1 and 10 instead of words. They can use any of these numbers in random order. The inflections will guide the conversation. Eliminating words makes it more challenging for the children to focus on intent and response, and to listen for variations in the voice that affect meaning.

A begins the exercise. For example: **A** begins by saying "9-4-1-3?"

Influenced by **A**'s inflection, **B** responds with "4-1-3?"

A answers: "9-4-1-3."

And so forth: **B** "9? 4-1-7!"

A "7!"

Don't be surprised if the children throw in words such as *oh* or *no* when they are truly caught up in the flow of the conversation, and in the meaning of the inflections.

Playing with Poetry

Explore the possibilities for inflection in the poem ***Do You Have a Minute, Santa?*** by Marilyn Smith.

Page 100

Poem Excerpts	Suggestions for Inflection
Do you have a minute, Santa, for a bit of a chat?	Use an upward inflection to communicate the question. If a downward inflection is used, this sentence becomes a statement.
We have lots and lots of questions about this and about that.	Use a falling inflection to indicate the completion of the thought. If the poet were to use an exclamation mark, it would change the meaning of the sentence. The reader would then use more vocal energy on the downward inflection, and add facial expression.
Do you like wearing red? Do you like eating cookies — Wherever you stop? Are you nervous on rooftops?	There are questions throughout this poem. Be cautious with the overall pitch through these lines, because there will be a tendency for the pitch to remain high throughout. Consider the context to vary the inflection on each question.
So let's talk dear Santa — PLEASE pick up the phone.	The circumflex inflection may communicate uncertainty about the possibility of actually talking to Santa. It may also mean hopefulness and anticipation of hearing Santa's voice on the phone. Use a downward inflection at the end of the poem to complete the presentation.

Remember that inflections reveal the intention of the speaker. Carefully consider the meaning, and allow inflections to occur naturally. Be careful not to deliberately exaggerate the voice in an effort to vary the inflections.

Do You Have a Minute, Santa?

by Marilyn Smith

Reader 1	Do you have a minute, Santa, for a bit of a chat?
Reader 2	We have lots and lots of questions about this and about that.
Reader 3 Reader 4	Do you like wearing red? Is it time for a change?
Reader 2 ALL	Would you rather wear blue — or would that be too strange?
Reader 4	Do you like eating cookies — wherever you stop?
Reader 2	Would you rather munch popcorn and sip soda pop?
Reader 1 Reader 3	Are you nervous on rooftops? Do you think you might fall?
Reader 2 Reader 4	Does Mrs. Claus worry? Do you give her a call?
Reader 2	Does your back start to ache?
Reader 3	Do your fingers get frozen from unloading presents that children have chosen?
Reader 4	Are some chimneys too narrow and dirty inside?
Reader 3	Do you sometimes get stuck — unable to slide?
Reader 2	Do you always make lists? Do you check them all twice?
Reader 1	Do you REALLY know who's naughty or nice?
Reader 4	The questions are endless.
Reader 3	The answers unknown.
Reader 1	So let's talk dear Santa —
Reader 2	PLEASE pick up the phone.

Reprinted from ***Early Literacy — A Seasonal Approach:*** *Enhancing a Balanced Literacy Program,* U-Otter-Read-It © 1999

Emphasis

Emphasis is a vocal expression technique to make important words and phrases stand out strongly. By simply changing the placement of emphasis, the meaning will change accordingly, resulting in different interpretations.

Symbol for **emphasis**:

____ Underline for emphasis

Stressing Emphasis

Use this activity to demonstrate how changes in emphasis also change meanings.

Place this phrase onto an overhead: I wish I had that toy.

Underline one word at a time in the sentence, and have the children say the phrase, placing emphasis on the underlined word.

Emphasizing different words in a sentence affects the overall meaning, and changes the way a listener responds to what is said.

- I wish I had that toy.
- I wish I had that toy.

  Emphasis on the word *I* personalizes the focus (*I* as opposed to *you*). By placing the emphasis on *I*, the speaker reveals a tone of desire, envy, or greed.

- I wish I had that toy.

  Emphasis on the word *wish* suggests a deep desire for the object.

- I wish I had that toy.

  Emphasis on the word *that* identifies a specific toy.

- I wish I had that toy.

  Emphasis on the word *toy* suggests a specific object — a toy as opposed to a bicycle.

After the children have tried several variations of this sentence, discuss observations of the change in meaning as a result of the shift in the placement of emphasis. Remember to consider the context, so that the placement of emphasis and the meaning are connected.

Techniques for Emphasis

Often, the operative word is emphasized by *stressing* the word. However, it is important to realize that other vocal expression techniques are equally effective for placing emphasis on an important word or phrase.

- **Volume** < >

  To use *volume* for emphasis, make the word louder or softer.

- **Inflection**

  To use *inflection* for emphasis, raise or lower the pitch of the voice.

- **Pause** /

  To use *pause* for emphasis, stop before and after the important word(s).

Emphasis can be placed on a word or a phrase by changing volume, inflection, pause, and stress.

As an example, vary the technique for emphasis on the word *room* in the following line: Get out of my room.

Get out of my room. (<)

Increasing volume to emphasize the word *room* adds a threatening element to the statement.

Get out of my room.

Using a downward inflection to emphasize the word *room* changes the statement to a command.

Get out of my / room.

Pausing before the word *room* indicates the speaker's impatience.

Playing with Poetry

Page 105

The poem ***Aunt Henney's Hairdo***, by Bridget Cohoe-Kenney, is perfect for practicing emphasis techniques.

Talk about Hair

Ask the children to share descriptions of unusual hair styles they have seen. They will likely talk about hair piled high in a big bun, or strange and unusual colours, spiky hair, or hair shaved into designs. Include balding hair as well! If necessary, bring in pictures to stimulate the discussion and build the vocabulary and background needed to perform ***Aunt Henney's Hairdo***.

Draw Aunt Henney's Hairdo

Introduce the poem by reading the title and asking for predictions about what would make Aunt Henney's hairdo so unique that someone would write a poem about it!

Read the poem to the children, while they draw their own versions of Aunt Henney's hairdo. Encourage them to write a few words to describe their pictures.

Read about Aunt Henney's Hairdo

Page 105

Provide each child with a copy of ***Aunt Henney's Hairdo***, and read the poem together. Ask the children to visualize their own version of Aunt Henney while they read, paying attention to words such as *curly*, *gold*, *hazel*, and *streaks* to help create the images of Aunt Henney.

Read the poem together again, this time with stronger emphasis on the descriptive words. The following example focuses on various vocal expression techniques for emphasis. You may want to mark your script with suggested symbols to assist with expression. For example:

It's / not / like the rest.

Poem	Suggestions for Emphasis
Aunt Henney's hairdo	Lift the word *hairdo* with inflection, rather than adding stress.
Is better than best,	Slightly stress the word *better* to indicate the best hairdo ever!
Even though Uncle thinks	Drop pitch on the word *Uncle* to indicate a male character.
It's / not / like the rest.	Pause before and after the word *not* to make it stand out.
Her curls are more curly, Her gold streaks more gold, Her browns are more hazel,	The qualities of her hairdo help us visualize what her hair really looks like. Emphasize these words with a slight stress.
Her reds are more bold.	Colour the words *curly*, *gold*, *hazel*, and *bold*.

Colouring, page 106

Page 105

Well, Uncle, he hates it	Stretch out the word *hates*, which intensifies the emotion of the word.
He's simply appalled.	Increase volume on the word *appalled* to strengthen his feelings of disgust and disbelief.
But I think he's jealous	Lift the word *I* to emphasize personal belief and interpretation of the situation.
'Cause Uncle is BALD.	The use of greater stress on the word *bald* is far more effective here than anywhere else in the poem, and creates a *punch line* effect. The last line is the most important, and needs to be timed and emphasized precisely if the audience is going to get the joke.

Perform the Poem

Opportunities to revisit text strengthen confidence and fluency.

Rehearse the poem by alternating readers until everyone has had the opportunity to read each part. In this way, the children develop a stronger sense of the total poem in terms of flow, content, and expressive qualities. Trading parts also gives the less confident readers the opportunity to work with the text several times before they are required to read solo.

Assign readers and rehearse the text. Consider having everyone's hair done up in a *wild* way. One child can represent the Uncle by wearing a hat with a bald cap underneath. When the final line is delivered, one of the other readers can lift the hat off the Uncle, revealing his bald head! Removing the hat on the word *BALD* is a dramatic way to physically emphasize the humour, creating a greater impact for the punch line.

> Remember that changing emphasis on a word changes the interpretation. Always consider the meaning within the context of the script, and decide which type of emphasis best lifts the word off the page and represents the author's intent.

Aunt Henney's Hairdo

by Bridget Cohoe-Kenney

Readers 1 & 3	Aunt Henney's hairdo
	Is better than best,
Readers 2 & 4	Even though Uncle thinks
	It's not like the rest.
Reader 3	Her curls are more curly,
Reader 2	Her gold streaks more gold,
Reader 1	Her browns are more hazel,
Reader 4	Her reds are more bold.
Readers 2 & 4	Well, Uncle, he hates it
	He's simply appalled.
Readers 1 & 3	But I think he's jealous
ALL	'Cause Uncle is BALD.

Used by permission of the poet

Colouring

Symbols for **colouring words**:

∼ Colouring words

⟷ Draw out the vowels

When introducing the concept of *colouring* to children, I always explain the difference between using pencil crayons to colour, and colouring words with the voice.

Colouring means to vocally enhance the meaning of the word. Colouring *animates* or lifts expressive words off the page through the use of various vocal expression techniques. For example, verbs, adverbs, and adjectives can be coloured through the use of pitch, inflection, and volume. Elongating (drawing out) the vowels, or stressing consonants, can colour the sounds in a word such as *freeze* to enhance the meaning.

Words and images stimulate the senses. The voice is an important tool for lifting the words off the page — highlighting them instead of allowing them to be flat and uninteresting. Writers are skilled in the craft of carefully selecting and organizing words to evoke specific responses from the audience. As intepreters, we must honour and give full value to the words that the writer has carefully chosen.

Readers respond to text on several levels.

Life experiences influence the reader's interpretation of the text. The ways in which the words are coloured are drawn from the reader's:

- Sensory awareness
- Confidence and skill with language
- Knowledge of the meaning of the words
- Emotional understanding of and connection to the text

Colouring Lively Words

Playing with words adds colour to the delivery and strengthens meaning.

To strengthen the concept of *colouring*, play with words, both physically and vocally.

Have the children say this sentence:

> This morning, I jumped out of bed, took a big stretch, and then stomped down the stairs.

Now explore the lively words in the sentence by doing the following exercise.

Say the word **jump** while jumping into the air. Notice how the voice goes up and then down.

- Say jump again, while jumping still higher into the air. Notice that the voice *jumps* to a higher pitch, in relation to the physical distance of the jump.
- Repeat the word *without* jumping. How can the same vocal effect be achieved? Aim to vocally re-create the *feeling* of the jump.

JUMP

Picture book authors and publishers use interesting fonts (typefaces) to provide clues about how a word can be said.

Say the word **stretch** while lengthening the body. Notice how the vowel elongates automatically.

- Ask the children to be even more physical by saying the word while stretching the arms up and out, as far as possible. How far can the word be *s-t-r-e-t-c-h-e-d*?
- Repeat the word *without* stretching. Did the word *feel* like a stretch? Aim to vocally re-create the physical feeling.

stretch

Say the word **stomp** while stomping the feet. Notice that the voice automatically responds by becoming heavy and strong.

- Repeat the word *without* stomping. Notice how the *face* still wants to respond. This adds texture to the word as the children recall the *feeling* of stomping.

STOMP

Now have the children say the sentence again, using *only* the voice to communicate the meaning of the words.

> This morning, I jumped out of bed, took a big stretch, and then stomped down the stairs.

Compare this delivery of the sentence to the initial delivery. Discuss how colouring enhances the meaning of the lively words. Remember to be careful that colouring words does not overshadow the flow of the sentence and detract from the overall meaning.

Caution
Avoid interrupting the flow of a phrase when colouring a word.

Colouring Noisy Words

Heighten the effect of *onomatopoeic* words by focusing on sound.

Say the word **buzz**. What part of the word can be coloured to capture the essence of buzzing? Focus on the fricative sound **z**, and lengthen the **zz**s to create the desired sound.

What sound is the focus in the word **thump**? To capture the essence of a thump, highlight and *explode* the final plosive **p**.

Exploring words through the senses strengthens connections to the meaning.

Vary the ways in which the children experience noisy words by using actual physical objects to demonstrate the sound quality of the word.

- Using a book, newspaper, or catalogue, *rustle* the pages. Say the word **rustle** in a way that captures the sound.
- Make a piece of chalk *squeal* across the blackboard. The children will immediately cover their ears. Say the word **squeal** so that it has the same effect. Did saying the word produce the same reaction? What has to happen to the voice to create that sensation of squealing chalk?

Encourage further exploration of other onomatopoeic words, identifying the parts of the word that need to be coloured to enhance the quality of the sound. Have the children consider the different vocal techniques they can change or control in order to capture the sound of a noisy word.

Colouring Sensory Words

Page 121

The poem ***All Kinds of Packages***, by Marilyn Smith, found in **Invitation to Readers Theatre**, provides opportunities for exploring and connecting to the senses. Examine text closely for descriptions that are especially stimulating to the five senses, and that lend themselves to vocal expression. Once sensory words are identified, the reader can explore ways to colour the words to stimulate the senses of the listeners. For example:

All kinds of packages,
under the tree,
sparkling, glistening,
calling to me.

Sensory focus on **sight**:
sparkling, *glistening*

There's boxes that rattle,
and clatter and creak,
but others are silent —
they don't make a peep.

Sensory focus on **sound**:
rattle, *clatter*, *creak*, *silent*, *peep*

Some parcels are squishy,
and some are quite hard.

Sensory focus on **touch**:
squishy, *hard*

Colouring Emotional Words

I once gave a script to a group of children, telling them that we would be *colouring* the words. Looking at the script, one child immediately piped up and asked for a red pencil crayon so that he could colour the word *furious*. When I asked how he would say the word, he responded, *"With lots of anger."*

When marking a script with symbols, use coloured pencils to remind readers of the attached emotion.

Emotional words are coloured by saying the word with feeling. The greater the feeling attached, the greater the impact on the audience. Saying the word *scared* without colouring has little effect, unless the speaker attaches the *feeling of being scared* to the vocal delivery.

Ask the children to think of something scary, and then to say the word **scared**. Practice this a few times before saying the following line, lifting the word *scared* off the page.

Readers attach their personal knowledge and background to words.

I was so scared when I saw that ghost.

How the audience responds will depend on the amount of *scariness* attached to the delivery. Encourage the children to feel the emotion as they communicate the entire statement. Used in context, the entire sentence can be *coloured* with the feeling, but the word *scared* will have increased impact.

Page 127

To further explore colouring emotional words, make a copy of the page of emotions, cut the words apart, and place them into a box. The children will draw a word at random, then use it in a line of text. For example:

- I was so ____________ when my brother did that.

Read the same line using different emotions. For example:

- I was so *frustrated* when my brother did that.
- I was so *shocked* when my brother did that.
- I was so *happy* when my brother did that.

Notice how the delivery of the entire line changes with different emotional words. What changes occur in posture and facial expression to emotionally colour the line? Draw attention to the importance of integrating the voice, the body, and the face to give full value to the emotion.

Colourific Words

Many words are *colourific words*, meaning that they are highly coloured, and can be vocally charged in a variety of ways. Use a combination of the voice, the body, and the face to fully explore colourific words. The way you colour a colourific word is determined by the context you wish to use.

- Lively words express physicality.
- Noisy words express sounds.
- Sensory words express senses.
- Emotional words express feelings.

SMASH

Consider the word **smash**.

Smash as a Lively Word

Say smash. Imagine smashing a tennis ball over a net, or smashing a baseball out to center field. How much energy goes into a smash? Say smash, adding vocal energy to the word.

Smash as a Noisy Word

Say smash. What part of the word can be coloured to capture the essence of a smash? Focus on the nasal sound **m**. Press the lips together as if you are smashing them like cymbals. What effect does this create? Focus on other sounds in smash — **s**, **a**, **sh**. Which is the most effective sound to colour?

Colourific words can be vocally charged in a variety of ways.

Smash as a Sensory Word

Say smash. Imagine hearing the sound of something smashing. How loud is a smashing sound? Is it high, low, loud, soft? Now say smash, capturing the qualities of a smashing sound.

Smash as an Emotional Word

Say smash. What feeling can be attached to a smash? Angry feelings can result in a smashing reaction; for example, a hand smashing down on a table. Colour the word smash with anger. Now consider the feeling of joy, as you applaud a smashing performance! Colour the word smash with joy.

Explore the following list of words in the same manner. Encourage the children to add to this list of colourific words.

boom	tingle	splash
swish	pop	low
ring	yawn	gloomy

Playing with Poetry

Sometimes, the way a word is printed on the page gives the reader a clue for colouring. Picture books often use a variety of fonts (typefaces) as visual cues to enhance oral expression.

Introduce the the poem ***School Song***, by Marilyn Smith. Use an overhead to draw attention to the way the words look on the page.

Page 112

Reading the poem line by line, experiment with different ways selected words can be coloured. Determine the focus that is most appropriate within the context of the poem (*lively*, *noisy*, *sensory*, *emotional*). Remember that other aspects of the word may be explored in addition to those suggestions listed below.

Buses **SCREECH**

Sensory word

Imagine hearing the sound of old school bus brakes *screeching* as the bus stops in front of the school. What kind of screech is produced? Is the sound high? Low? Soft? Loud? Short? Long? Add this effect to the phrase as you focus on colouring the word *screech.*

Zippers *zzzzzip*

Noisy word

Focus on the sound of a zipper. If you can, actually zip some zippers! What part of the word can be extended to capture the zipping sound? Focus on the fricative **z** sound. Imagine how the teeth of the zipper need to come together when zippers are zipped. Likewise, the teeth need to be close together to produce the **z** sound.

Feet **hustle**

Lively word

Say the word *hustle*, while hustling quickly around the room. Notice how the pace of the word relates to the action of hustling. Is hustling energetic or lazy? When you say the word, match the vocal energy to the physical energy expended in hustling.

Children **laugh**

Emotional word

What causes laughter? Feelings of giddiness, excitement, or hilarity can provoke this response. Colour the word *laugh*, attaching an emotional context to the delivery.

> Remember that colouring words gives extra life to the text. The expressive technique of colouring makes the reading experience more enjoyable for both speaker and listener.

School Song

by Marilyn Smith

Reader 1	Buses SCREECH
Reader 2	Bells are RUNG
Reader 3	Teachers greet
ALL	Day's begun.
Reader 4	Voices CHATTER
Reader 5	Chalk squeaks
Reader 6	Paint splatters
Readers 2 & 6	Chairs CREAK.
Reader 5	Mouths slurp
Reader 2	Teeth CRUNCH
Reader 1	Tummies burp
Readers 3 & 4	Must be lunch!
Reader 6	Pages rustle
Reader 1	Pencils scratch
Reader 3	Feet hustle
Readers 1 & 5	Children laugh.
Reader 2	Zippers zzzzzip
Reader 4	Boots THUMP
Reader 5	Light-switches flip flip
ALL	Day's done!

Reprinted from ***Invitation to Readers Theatre:*** *A Guidebook for using Readers Theatre to celebrate holidays and special events throughout the year,* U-Otter-Read-It © 1997

Volume

Symbols for **volume**:

< Louder

> Softer

Volume is the increase or decrease of sound resulting from the intensity of vocal fold vibration. Volume levels are generally categorized as *soft*, *medium*, or *loud*. A voice that has variations between *soft* and *loud* volume adds greater expression and interest to a selection.

Volume vs. pitch

Remember that *loud* and *soft* refer to changes in volume, while *high* and *low* refer to changes in pitch.

Volume Variations

Speaking **LOUDLY** is not the same as *screaming*. In order to create a **loud** voice, the muscles of exhalation — the abdominal muscles — must be used to energize the sound. The push does not come from the throat muscles. Remember to use good vocal hygiene when working with volume extremes.

Vocal Hygiene, page 17

Speaking *softly* is not the same as *whispering*. A whisper in performance is difficult to hear. A *stage whisper*, on the other hand, can be heard clearly. A stage whisper has the breathy quality of a whisper, but is still vocalized — the vocal folds vibrate so that the sound can be projected.

Understanding extreme volume levels

It is important to remember that volume isn't just *loud* or *soft* — there are different levels between the two extremes. For example, lines of text that are punctuated with exclamation marks can be delivered effectively when the reader *builds* volume through the line in order to emphasize the final word. However, it is just as effective to *reduce* volume through a line to bring attention to a word, mood, or feeling at the end. Changes in volume are affected by interpretation, personal experience, and knowledge of the content.

Interpretation gives clues about the most effective volume level.

***Bedtime,* Invitation to Munsch**

Bibliography, page 121

Below are examples of increasing or decreasing volume through a line of text. Note the extended volume symbol above the second line to indicate the gradual, controlled increase or decrease in volume.

INCREASE

Example of building or increasing volume through a line:

Above the earth, up through the stars,

I'll travel away to a place like MARS!

DECREASE

Example of reducing or decreasing volume through a line:

Oh no, there's footsteps — someone's coming!

I'll pretend to sleep or something!

Volume Control

Physical control is required to gradually increase or decrease volume through a line or stanza. There will be a gradual pressure of the stomach muscles as the sound increases or decreases smoothly.

Breathing, page 34

12345678

Ask the children to stand in proper alighment, placing their hands on the stomach area. Count aloud from 1 to 8, building in volume as the numbers increase. How does the abdominal area feel as the volume increases? Now count from 8 to 1, decreasing the volume as the numbers decrease. What happens in the abdominal area?

Abdominal press, page 39

Remind the children to increase *volume*, not pitch, and ensure that they are supporting their voices with the *abdominal press*, **not** the throat. Repeat this exercise several times to achieve proper support for the voice.

The Control Button

To increase awareness of physical control, have the children stand in proper alignment, with the hands placed gently on the stomach — more specifically, on the belly button, or *volume control.*

Ask the children to take in a deep breath, and to release an **awww** (as in *ball*) sound. Allow the breath to diminish completely before stopping the flow of sound. Now ask them to *increase* the volume as they release the **awww** sound. What did they feel? Repeat the exercise, *decreasing* the volume as they release the **awww** sound. Note the difference between loud and soft.

The children will observe the feeling of pressure on the abdominal muscles to support an increase in volume, and less pressure as volume decreases.

The Volume Scale

Within the range of loud to soft, there are endless possibilities for subtleties in volume shifts. To assist children in understanding and exploring these subtleties, use a *volume scale.*

Create a visual scale with numbers from 1 to 8, with 1 representing soft volume and 8 representing loud volume — similar to the volume control on a stereo sound system.

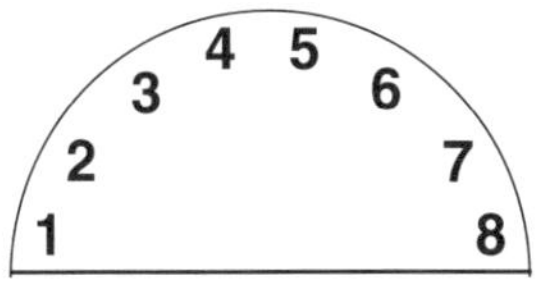

Volume Scale

Ask the children to count aloud from 1 to 8, *building* in volume as the numbers increase. Guide the children by pointing to the numbers on the volume scale. Then have the children count from 8 to 1, *reducing* the volume as the numbers decrease. Guide the children by pointing to the numbers on the volume scale.

Now point to any number on the volume scale, asking the children to match the appropriate volume to the number indicated. Point in between numbers to encourage them to explore even greater subtleties in volume.

Challenge the children even further by creating a scale up to 10 or 12. Can they increase volume with smaller shifts between the numbers? To do this effectively, children will experience very slight shifts between the volume levels.

The children will become aware of the *range* of volumes available to them when they use volume as an expressive technique.

Using the Volume Symbol

The volume symbol can be used in a number of ways. For example, it can go *above* a line to indicate a gradual increase or decrease through the line:

Visual cues enhance the understanding and use of volume.

Mortimer's voice is tremendously loud!

Or the volume symbol can go *beside* a line, indicating whether the voice is generally soft or loud through the line:

< It's as loud as loud can be!

> Like the footsteps of a caterpillar crawling.

To assist children with a more specific level of volume, a number related to the volume scale can be placed inside the symbol:

<8 It's as loud as loud can be!

2> Like the footsteps of a caterpillar crawling.

Page 118

Playing with Poetry

Mortimer's Voice, by Marilyn Smith and Helen Raczuk, is a perfect poem for exploring the subtle changes between a soft and a loud voice.

To allow for individual interpretation, the following suggestions for volume are listed *without* the specific volume symbols. As an exercise, determine which volume numbers would be most appropriate for the following lines, and mark the script accordingly.

Poem Excerpts	Suggestions for Volume
Mortimer's voice is tremendously loud!	Consider the meaning of the word *tremendous*. How loud is that on a scale of 1 to 8? Building the volume through the line may capture the strength of his voice, while an even use of a loud volume throughout the line may reduce the importance of the final two words.
He has no trouble being heard in a crowd.	How can one voice carry over the sound of a group of voices? Use the abdominal press to gain additional power for the voice.
It's like 17 firetrucks screeching through the night,	Imagine the sound of 17 firetruck sirens. How loud is that on the volume scale? *Screeching* indicates a higher pitch level. Use both pitch and volume to create this effect.
Or a freight train rumbling out of sight!	What kind of voice captures the size of a freight train? Perhaps using a louder voice that is lower in pitch will create variety and contrast from the previous line. In addition, the train *rumbles out of sight*. Decreasing volume through the line helps to convey that image. Can you decrease the volume without losing the effect of *loudness*?

Pitch, page 90

But what if —	Using a medium volume and a long pause here helps to prepare the audience for a shift in ideas.	**Pause and Phrasing**, page 78
Mortimer's voice was terrifically gentle?	How quiet is a *terrifically gentle* voice on the volume scale? Reducing the volume throughout this line helps to focus the audience's attention on the words *terrifically gentle*.	
Like the scratching of a yellow pencil Or the purr of a kitten on your lap Or water dripping from a tap.	How quiet are these sounds? Listen to a pencil scratching on paper. Imagine other gentle sounds. How would these sounds rate on the volume scale? Use a variety of soft voices for these lines, adding colouring and inflections to enhance the delivery.	Remember that the audience must still be able to hear the words. A stage whisper may be used here. **Colouring**, page 106 **Inflection**, page 96
Just think. How would that be?	Use optimum pitch, medium volume, and a long pause to connect with the audience, and to set up the punch line.	**Pitch**, page 90
BORING!	Use volume to emphasize this word for the most dramatic effect.	

Remember that increasing volume should not directly affect the pitch of the voice, because the force behind volume is controlled by the breath and not the vocal folds. Use changes in volume to communicate mood, climax, feelings, and meaning.

Mortimer's Voice

by Marilyn Smith and Helen Raczuk

Reader 1	Mortimer's voice is tremendously loud!
Reader 3	He has no trouble being heard in a crowd.
Reader 4	It's like 17 firetrucks screeching through the night,
Reader 2	or a freight train rumbling out of sight!
Reader 4	It can shatter a drinking glass to pieces,
Reader 3	like 30 grade ones going out for recess.
ALL	It's as loud as loud can be!
Reader 2	But, what if —
Reader 1	Mortimer's voice was terrifically gentle?
Reader 3	Like the scratching of a yellow pencil
Reader 4	or the purr of a kitten on your lap
Reader 2	or water dripping from a tap.
Reader 3	Like the footsteps of a caterpillar crawling
Reader 1	or the sound of a leaf, as it's falling?
Reader 2	Just think. How *would* that be?
ALL	**BORING!**

Reprinted from ***Invitation to Munsch:*** *A Guidebook for use with selected works of Canadian Author Robert Munsch*, U-Otter-Read-It © 1996

A Vocal Wrap-Up

Proper voice production, combined with effective use of vocal expression techniques, enables us to achieve our full vocal potential. By reading literature aloud in a creative, encouraging, and enjoyable atmosphere, children have the freedom to explore their voices, and to develop greater confidence. Speaking effectively is an essential and valuable life skill, and the gains are life-long.

Voices that achieve full vocal potential are flexible, expressive, energetic, sincere, clear, and pleasant. These qualities are further defined as:

Qualities of an effective voice:
- Flexibility
- Expressiveness
- Energy
- Sincerity
- Clarity
- Pleasantness

Flexible — A voice that is flexible adapts easily to any speaking situation or environment. A flexible voice enables us to speak appropriately to a friend at a circus as well as a friend at a funeral.

Energetic — A voice that is vibrant, powered by the breath and the desire to be heard, captures and holds the attention of the listener.

Expressive — A voice that is modulated with the techniques of expression, including pitch, pace, pause, phrasing, inflection, emphasis, and colouring, is able to lift meaning off the page with greater skill.

Clear — A voice that is articulate receives greater listener response to the text. When words are pronounced clearly, there is little risk of misunderstanding.

Sincere — A voice that communicates naturally and sincerely is most desirable. When the listener believes the message, the connection between the listener and the speaker is genuine.

Pleasant — A voice that has a pleasing, resonant quality is more likely to hold the interest of the listener, making the communication experience more satisfying.

These are the goals we wish to achieve as we aim to create powerful vocal instruments.

Page 128

Children can evaluate their voices by using the *Vocal Evaluation Checklist* on page 128. This checklist gives children an opportunity to self-monitor elements of proper voice production and vocal expression as they work to achieve their full vocal potential.

Voice work is essential when exploring Readers Theatre. The voice is the tool that gives life to the words. Once the words are lifted off the page, they can be enhanced to increase the impact of the message. Facial expressions and physical gesturing are additional techniques that complete the speaker's instrument — the connection of voice, face, and body. These components, along with the theatrical conventions of Readers Theatre, will be the focus of **An Invitation to Perform Readers Theatre**, the companion to this guidebook.

A Final Invitation

The choice of material for vocal exploration is endless. I have assisted you with examples and references to the U-Otter-Read-It books used and listed throughout this guidebook. Other collections for you to discover are listed in the bibliography. I invite you to be creative with literature as you continue your vocal exploration of Readers Theatre.

My Otter Notes

Resources

This section contains the following resources:
- Bibliography
- Reproducibles

Bibliography

Poetry Collections for Use with Readers Theatre

365 Nursery Rhymes in Color. New York: Gallery Books, 1972.

Booth, David. **Til All the Stars Have Fallen: Canadian Poems for Children**. Toronto: Kids Can Press Ltd., 1989.

Dahl, Roald. **Revolting Rhymes**. New York: Bantam Skylark, 1986.

Downie, Mary Alice & Barbara Robertson. **The New Wind Has Wings: Poems from Canada**. Toronto: Oxford University Press, 1984.

Fitch, Sheree. **Toes In My Nose**. Canada: Doubleday Canada Ltd, 1987.

Hale, Glorya. **Read-Aloud Poems for Young People**. New York: Black Dog & Leventhal Publishers, 1997.

Lansky, Bruce. **A Bad Case of the Giggles.** Deephaven, MN: Meadowbrook Press, 1994.

_________. **Kids Pick the Funniest Poems**. Deephaven, MN: Meadowbrook Press, 1991.

_________. **Miles of Smiles**. Deephaven, MN: Meadowbrook Press, 1998.

_________. **Poetry Party**. Deephaven, MN: Meadowbrook Press, 1996.

Lee, Dennis. **Garbage Delight**. Toronto: Macmillan of Canada, 1979.

_________. **Alligator Pie**. Toronto: Macmillan of Canada, 1974.

_________. **Jelly Belly**. Toronto: Macmillan of Canada, 1983.

_________. **The Ice Cream Store**. Toronto: HarperCollins Publishers Ltd, 1991.

Molnar, Gwen. **Animal Rap and Far-Out Fables**. Victoria, B.C.: Beach Holme Publishing Ltd., 1996.

Moss, Jeff. **The Butterfly Jar**. New York: Bantam Books, 1989.

_________. **The Sesame Street Book of Poetry**. Toronto: Random House, 1992.

_________. **The Other Side of the Door**. New York: Bantam Books, 1991.

Prelutsky, Jack. **The Random House Book of Poetry for Children**. New York: Random House, 1983.

_________. **A Pizza the Size of the Sun**. New York: Scholastic Inc., 1996.

_________. **The New Kid on the Block**. New York: Scholastic Inc., 1984.

_________. **Something Big Has Been Here**. New York: Greenwillow Books, 1990.

Rogers, Linda & Rick Van Krugel. **Brown Bag Blues**. Victoria: Studio 123, 1991.

Rosen, Michael. **Poems for the Very Young**. New York: Kingfisher Books, 1993.

Silverstein, Shel. **A Light in the Attic**. New York: Harper & Row Publishers, 1981.

_________. **Falling Up**. New York: HarperCollins Publishers, 1996.

_________. **Where the Sidewalk Ends**. New York: Harper & Row Publishers, 1974.

Simmie, Lois. **An Armadillo Is Not a Pillow**. Saskatoon, Saskatchewan: Western Producer Prairie Books, 1986.

_________. **Auntie's Knitting a Baby**. Saskatoon, Saskatchewan: Western Producer Prairie Books, 1987.

Westcott, Nadine Bernard. **Never Take a Pig to Lunch**. New York: Orchard Books, 1994.

Tongue Twisters & Twister Tales

Atwood, Margaret. **Princess Prunella and the Purple Peanut**. Toronto: Key Porter Kids, 1995.

Brandreth, Gyles. **The Biggest Tongue Twister Book in the World**. New York: Sterling Publishing Co. Inc, 1978.

Charney, Steve. **Six Thick Thumbs: A Tongue-Twisting Tale**. U.S.A.: Troll Associates, 1994.

Cole, Joanna & Stephanie Calmenson. **Six Sick Sheep: 101 Tongue Twisters**. New York: Scholastic Inc., 1993.

Cookson, Paul. **Let's Twist Again!** London, England: Macmillan Children's Books, 2000.

Karshner, Roger. **You Said A Mouthful**. Toluca Lake, CA: Dramaline Publications, 1993.

Obligado, Lilian. **Faint Frogs Feeling Feverish**. New York: Picture Puffins, 1986.

Rosenbloom, Joseph & Mike Artell. **The Little Giant Book of Tongue Twisters**. New York: Sterling Publishing Co. Inc, 1999.

Rosenbloom, Joseph. **World's Toughest Tongue Twisters**. New York: Sterling Publishing Co. Inc, 1987.

Schwartz, Alvin. **Busy Buzzing Bumblebees and Other Tongue Twisters**. U.S.A.: HarperTrophy, 1982.

Readers Theatre

Braun, Win & Carl Braun. **Readers Theatre for Young Children**. Calgary, AB: Braun & Braun Educational Enterprises Ltd., 1998.

Coger, Leslie Irene & Melvin R. White. **Readers Theatre Handbook**. U.S.A.: Scott Foresman and Co., 1982.

Dixon, Neill, Anne Davies & Colleen Politano. **Learning with Readers Theatre**. Winnipeg, Manitoba: Peguis Publishers, 1996.

Hill, Susan. **Readers Theatre: Performing the Text**. Winnipeg, Manitoba: Peguis Publishers, 1995.

Kline, Suzy. **The Herbie Jones Reader's Theatre**. New York: G. P. Putnam's Sons, 1992.

Laughlin, Mildred Knight & Kathy Howard Latrobe. **Readers Theatre for Children**. Englewood, CO: Teacher Ideas Press, 1990.

Raczuk, Helen & Marilyn Smith. **Invitation to Munsch: A Guidebook for use with selected works of Canadian Author Robert Munsch**. Spruce Grove, Alberta: U-Otter-Read-It, 1996.

Raczuk, Helen & Marilyn Smith. **Invitation to Readers Theatre: A Guidebook for using Readers Theatre to celebrate holidays and special events throughout the year**. Spruce Grove, Alberta: U-Otter-Read-It, 1997.

_________. **Invitation to Readers Theatre: Celebrating Stories of our Canadian Heritage**. Spruce Grove, Alberta: U-Otter-Read-It, 1998.

_________. **Early Literacy — A Seasonal Approach: Enhancing a Balanced Literacy Program**. Spruce Grove, Alberta: U-Otter-Read-It, 1999.

White, Mel. **Readers Theatre Anthology**. Colorado Springs, CO: Meriwether Publishing Ltd., 1993.

Voice Production

Anderson, Virgil A. **Training the Speaking Voice**. 3rd ed. London: Oxford University Press, 1977.

Andrews, Moya L. **Voice Therapy for Children**. San Diego: Singular Publishing Group, Inc., 1998.

Glenn, Ethel C., Phillip J. Glenn & Sandra Forman. **Your Voice and Articulation**. Needham Heights, MA: Allyn & Bacon, 1998.

Linklater, Kristin. **Freeing the Natural Voice**. 2nd ed. New York: Drama Book Publishers., 1985.

Mayer, Lyle V. **Fundamentals of Voice & Diction**. 10th ed. Dubuque, IA: Wm. C. Brown Communications, Inc., 1994.

Morrison, Malcolm. **Clear Speech: Practical Speech Correction and Voice Improvement**. 2nd ed. London: A & C Black Publishers, Ltd., 1989.

Rodenburg, Patsy. **The Right to Speak: Working with the Voice**. New York: Routledge, Chapman & Hall, 1993.

Showers, Paul. **How You Talk**. New York: HarperTrophy, 1992.

Additional Resources

Barker, Sarah. **The Alexander Technique**. New York: Bantam Books, 1991.

Booth, David & Bill Moore. **Poems Please! Sharing Poetry with Children**. Markham, Ontario: Pembroke Publishers Ltd., 1988.

Jones, James Earl & Penelope Niven. **Voices and Silences**. New York: Macmillan Publishing Co., 1993.

LaRoche, Loretta. **Relax — You May Only Have a Few Minutes Left**. New York: Villard Books, 1998.

Larrick, Nancy. **Let's Do a Poem: Introducing Poetry to Children**. New York: Delacorte Press, 1991.

Novelly, Maria C. **Theatre Games for Young Performers**. Colorado Springs, CO: Meriwether Publishing Ltd., 1985.

Scher, Anna & Charles Verrall. **100+ Ideas for Drama**. London: Heinemann Educational Books, 1988.

Tanner, Fran Averett. **Creative Communication**. 3rd ed. Caldwell, ID.: Clark Publishing Co., 1985.

Yordon, Judy E. **Roles in Interpretation**. 4th ed. Boston: McGraw-Hill College, 1999.

Vocal Hygiene —
How To Take Care of Your Voice

- Drink lots of water to keep the voice moist.
- Be careful not to **scream** or **cheer**.
- Avoid **shouting** across the playground. Move closer to talk.
- Be careful not to **clench** your jaw, or move it from side to side.
- Slow down your speech! Use pauses, so you can take in lots of air.
- Be careful not to clear your throat **roughly**. Swallow, drink water, or use a gentle little cough to clear the throat.
- Remember not to **overuse** your voice when you are tired or sick.
- Remember to warm up vocally before a presentation.
- When playing with character voices, avoid **pushing** your voice too high or too low.
- Avoid **straining** your voice when talking in noisy places.
- Avoid gargling! Drink water!
- Avoid **forcing** your voice when you are singing.
- If your throat **hurts** when you talk, always let a parent or a teacher know.

For use with *The Breathing Maze* on page 39 and *A-Maze-ing!* on page 52

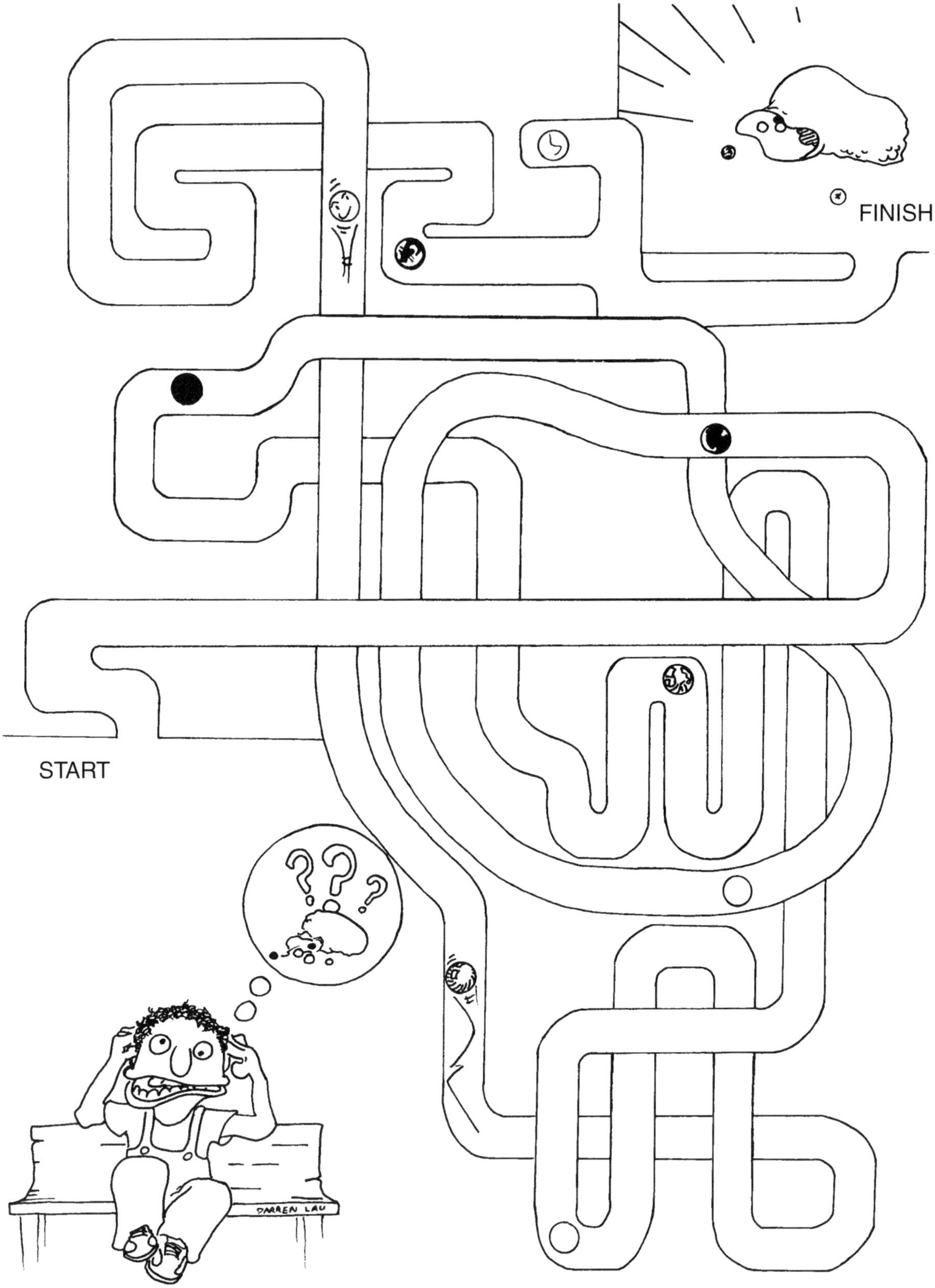

For use with *The Chinese Fortune Teller Exercise* on page 55

1. Start with a square piece of paper, about 18 cm x 18 cm, and find the center.

2. Fold corners in to meet at the middle (left-hand diagram). When the folds are done, the paper will look like the right-hand diagram.

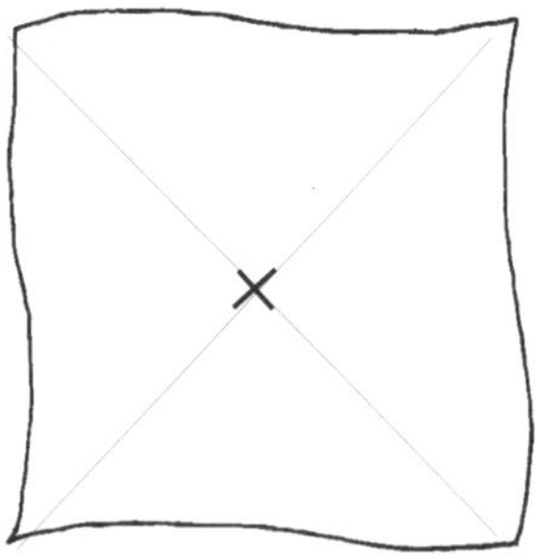

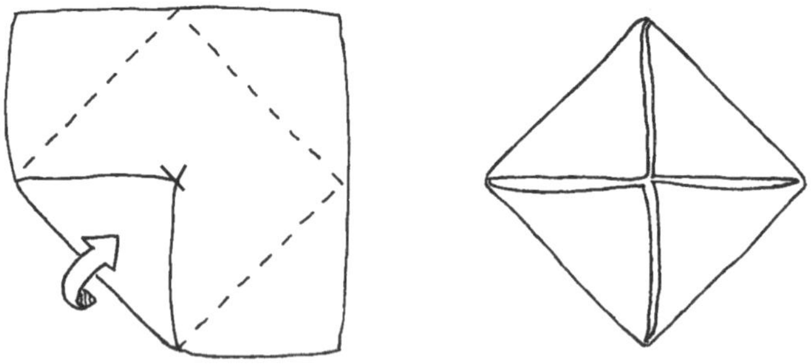

3. Turn the folded square over, and again fold each corner in to the middle (left-hand diagram). When the folds are done, the paper will look like the right-hand diagram.

4. Now fold the top half of the square over to meet the bottom half.

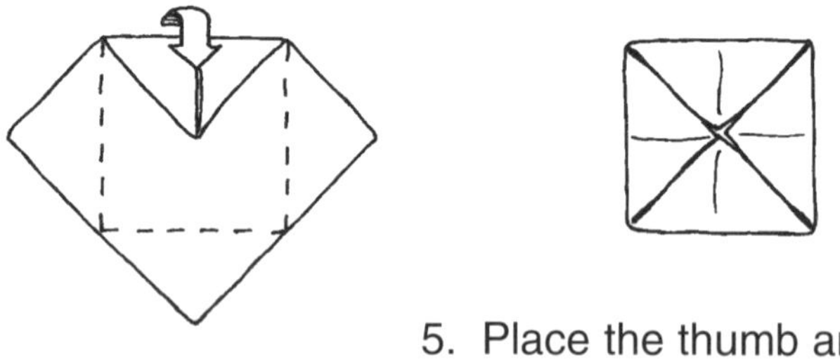

5. Place the thumb and index finger of each hand under the flaps. Bring fingers and thumbs together to form the Chinese Fortune Teller.

For use with exercises on pages 97, 109, and 127

Emotions

Curious	Sad
Angry	Disbelieving
Frustrated	Exhausted
Worried	Concerned
Thoughtful	Disappointed
Excited	Upset
Convincing	Disgusted
Grumpy	Kind
Shocked	Surprised
Caring	Frightened
Terrified	Tense
Happy	Arrogant
Mischievous	Depressed
Lonely	Dreamy
Clueless	Disapproving
Horrified	Delighted

Refer to *A Vocal Wrap-Up* on page 119

Vocal Evaluation Checklist

U-Otter Hear My Voice!

Name: ______________________________

When I performed my script:	☹	→			☺
• **I felt relaxed.**	**1**	**2**	**3**	**4**	**5**
• **I placed my body in proper alignment.**	**1**	**2**	**3**	**4**	**5**
• **I breathed deeply without the use of my shoulders.**	**1**	**2**	**3**	**4**	**5**
• **I avoided tension in my throat.**	**1**	**2**	**3**	**4**	**5**
• **I pulled the sound out from the back of my throat.**	**1**	**2**	**3**	**4**	**5**
• **I projected to the back of the room without strain.**	**1**	**2**	**3**	**4**	**5**
• **I used a variety of expression techniques:**					
• **I varied my pitch.**	**1**	**2**	**3**	**4**	**5**
• **I used pauses.**	**1**	**2**	**3**	**4**	**5**
• **I emphasized important words.**	**1**	**2**	**3**	**4**	**5**
• **I used inflections for meaning.**	**1**	**2**	**3**	**4**	**5**
• **I varied the pace.**	**1**	**2**	**3**	**4**	**5**
• **I built to a climax.**	**1**	**2**	**3**	**4**	**5**
• **I used facial expression.**	**1**	**2**	**3**	**4**	**5**

Directions for use: Consider how well you remembered the above statements by circling the number that you think best shows how you did. For example, if you placed your body comfortably in proper alignment during your performance, you will circle 4 or 5. If you slouched or lost your balance because your feet were too close together, you will circle 1 or 2 for the alignment statement.

My comments:

"What an inspiring workshop. I have used Readers Theatre, but didn't know how to get the potential for excitement and engagement!" — A. Nordby, Vancouver, B.C.

READERS THEATRE

An Early Invitation to Readers Theatre

Content focus: Primary

A wide range of original scripts, based on favourite stories and themes, will be read and developed in this interactive seminar aimed at primary grades.
Participants will:

- Explore techniques to promote expressive, independent reading
- Explore a variety of instructional strategies to strengthen literacy skills
- Explore connections to other curriculum disciplines

An Otter Invitation to Readers Theatre

Content focus: Upper Elementary & Junior High

Drawing on scripts based on folk tales, stories, and legends from around the world, participants will:

- Develop strategies to reinforce literacy skills
- Learn techniques to guide students toward script development
- Explore connections to other curriculum disciplines, and connect to basic ideals and goals

"The workshop was great! I now have an idea of where to start with my class and what areas of readers theatre that I can focus on to develop my students' oral reading skills." — Jennifer Pryor, Abbotsford, B.C.

EARLY LITERACY

Early Literacy: Stories, Strategies, and Scripts

Content focus: ECS & Primary

In this interactive workshop, participants will:

- Explore picture books as a tool for developing literacy skills
- Develop a list of great titles to enhance balanced literacy programs
- Build a repertoire of practical teaching ideas for introducing, developing, and extending literature in the classroom

"I just started teaching in resource room, and I think this type of presentation would be excellent. Students in resource deserve good literature." — D. Blackmer, Medicine Hat, Alberta

MUSIC AND LANGUAGE

Poetry, Music, and Rhyme

Content focus: Primary & Upper Elementary

This interactive session will provide participants with a wide range of tools and resources to build on language and music skills.

- Explore ways to build on poetry to extend writing skills
- Strengthen literacy skills through rhyme and rhythm
- Sing and revisit familiar and new childhood songs and rhymes

READ-IT **U-Otter-Read-It**

Professional Development Workshops

We are pleased to design workshops specific to the needs of your staff, PD organization, or conference. Please visit **http://www.uotter.com** for updates about workshops in your area, and to learn about many more topics available for your professional development event!

Contact information:
Phone: **780-962-9854** • Fax: **780-962-9882**
Email: **workshops@uotter.com**

"Very well organized. Fun activities with all the theory to back them up. We hope to try this with 'challenged adults'." — C. Arnold, Edmonton, Alberta

VOCAL EXPRESSION

The Teacher's Voice

Content focus: All levels

In this practical workshop, participants will:

- Gain an understanding of how the voice works by examining voice production, including breathing, resonance, and oral muscularity
- Learn to use exercises to overcome habitual vocal and physical barriers that interfere with the freeing of the *natural* voice
- Increase their ability to evaluate personal voice difficulties

STORYTELLING

The Teacher as Storyteller

Content focus: All levels

In this practical workshop, participants will:

- Focus on improving their storytelling, oral reading ability, and overall vocal and physical expression
- Develop vocal expression techniques such as pause, pace, phrasing, emphasis, inflection, and modulation
- Discover ways to increase their *vocal impact* on the listener

"Good attention to the variety of ways of working with a script. I think this may be a good activity for Eng. As Additional Language kids." — R. Pile, London, England

We are interested in the following title(s)

____

____

for a session on __________ (date)
at __________ (place)

Contact Name __________
Phone __________ Fax __________
Email __________
Other __________

____

U-OTTER READ-IT™
Educational Resources Ltd.

Place your order on the web: www.uotter.com *or* orders@uotter.com

Phone your order: 780-962-9854 • **Fax** your order: 780-962-9882

Mail your order: U-Otter-Read-It, 11 Miller Place,
Spruce Grove, Alberta, Canada T7X 2N1

Mail to:
Contact
Address

City
Province
PCode
Phone
Fax
Email

Bill to:
Contact
Address

City
Province
PCode
Phone
Fax
Email

Purchase Order #	Approved by:	Cheque Enclosed:

Item #	**Qty**	**Item Description**	**Price**	**Total**
001 MTG		***Invitation to Munsch***, by Raczuk & Smith	$22.95	
001 MOT		Set of 5 overhead Readers Theatre transparencies to accompany *Invitation to Munsch*	$ 7.95	
Munsch Set		Munsch teacher guide + overhead transparency set	$28.00	
002 RTG		***Invitation to Readers Theatre***, a Guidebook for using Readers Theatre to celebrate holidays and special events throughout the year, by Raczuk & Smith	$22.95	
002-BLM		Blackline Masters to accompany *Invitation to Readers Theatre*	$ 7.95	
AR-002		***Animal Rap and Far Out Fables***, by Gwen Molnar	$ 7.95	
GREEN Set		*Readers Theatre* (holidays) + Blackline Masters + *Animal Rap*	$35.00	
003 RTG2		***Invitation to Readers Theatre***, Celebrating Stories of our Canadian Heritage, by Raczuk & Smith	$22.95	
004 ELS		***Early Literacy — A Seasonal Approach***, by Raczuk & Smith	$22.95	
004-BLM		Blackline Masters to accompany *Early Literacy*	$ 9.95	
PURPLE Set		*Early Literacy* book + Blackline Masters	$30.00	
005 VRT		***A Vocal Invitation to Readers Theatre***, by S. Konrad	$29.95	
		Readers Theatre performance packages:		
Cobbler		*The Cobbler and His Guest*	$ 9.95	
Legend		*A Legend for Christmas* (2 versions)	$ 9.95	
Night		*Night Before Christmas*	$ 9.95	
Thousand		*Feeding Five Thousand* (loaves & fishes story)	$ 9.95	
Shepherds		*The Shepherds Story*	$ 9.95	

Shipping & Handling

Order:	**Add:**
Up to $30	$4.00
$31-$50	$5.00
$51-$100	8%
$101- $500 . . .	7%
Over $500 . . .	5%

Subtotal ______
Shipping & Handling ______
G.S.T. ______
TOTAL Order ______